THE CHANGING
OF THE GUARD

Other books by George Grant

Bringing in the Sheaves:
Transforming Poverty into Productivity, 1985

The Dispossessed:
Homelessness in America, 1986

In the Shadow of Plenty:
Biblical Principles of Welfare and Poverty, 1986

LifeLight:
The Bible and the Sanctity of Human Life, 1987

To the Work:
Ideas for Biblical Charity, 1987

Achan in the Camp:
Moral Compromise in the Church, 1987

The Big Lie:
The Scandal of Planned Parenthood, 1987

Rebuilding the Walls:
A Biblical Strategy for Restoring America's Greatness, 1987
[with Peter Waldron]

A Catechism of Occultism:
A Christian Response to Dungeons and Dragons, 1987
[with Peter Leithart]

Powerful Living:
The Bible and the Victorious Christian Life, 1987
[edited by George Grant]

THE CHANGING OF THE GUARD

Biblical Blueprints for Political Action

George Grant

Dominion Press
Ft. Worth, Texas

Published by Dominion Press
7112 Burns Street, Ft. Worth, Texas 76118

Typesetting by Thoburn Press, Tyler, Texas

Printed in the United States of America

Unless otherwise noted, all Scripture quotations are from the New King James Version of the Bible, copyrighted 1984 by Thomas Nelson, Inc., Nashville, Tennessee.

Library of Congress Catalog Card Number 87-070996

ISBN 0-930462-27-0

To David Dunham
a friend indeed
and
to Karen Grant
a friend in deed.

When the righteous are in authority, the people rejoice; but when a wicked man rules, the people groan.

Proverbs 29:2

TABLE OF CONTENTS

ACKNOWLEDGEMENTS

"Writing is painfully easy," Gene Fowler was wont to say, "All you do is stare at a blank sheet of paper until drops of blood form on your forehead."

Fortunately, a number of kind-hearted souls coaxed me through the agony and ecstasy of this book project, and as a result, my hemoglobin loss was minimal. David Dunham, Jim Jordan, Kemper Crabb, Frank Marshall, Gary DeMar, Dave Marshall, and Brian Martin all afforded me transfusions of wisdom, encouragement, and joy when I most needed them. Kathe Salazar, J. D. McWilliams, and Suzanne Martin mopped my brow and nursed me along, all the while taking care of business and holding down the fort. Great thanks is here given to each of these dear friends and fellow-workers in the Kingdom.

Of course, even with the valiant efforts of all these, completion of this book still would have been impossible were it not for the blood of my blood, the love of my love: Karen, Joel, Joanna, and Jesse. No expression of gratitude can even begin to approach adequacy. And so:

"I thank my God always concerning you for the grace of God which was given to you by Christ Jesus, that you were enriched in everything by Him in all utterance and all knowledge, even as the testimony of Christ was confirmed in you, so that you come short in no gift, eagerly waiting for the revelation of our Lord Jesus Christ, who will also confirm you to the end, that you may be blameless in the day of our Lord Jesus Christ. God is faithful, by whom you were called into the fellowship of His Son, Jesus Christ our Lord" (1 Corinthians 1:4-9).

Writing may be "painfully easy," but with the cup of graciousness that God, family, and friends have afforded me, the "painful" part was truly "eased"!

Epiphany Sunday, 1987
Humble, Texas

EDITOR'S INTRODUCTION
by Gary North

Jesus answered, "My Kingdom is not of this world. If My Kingdom were of this world, My servants would fight, so that I should not be delivered to the Jews; but now My Kingdom is not from here" (John 18:36).

Few passages in the Bible are misinterpreted as often in our day as this one. The only other one that occurs to me is: "Judge not, that you be not judged" (Matthew 7:1).

Whenever a speaker begins to argue that Christians have a responsibility to work to build God's Kingdom on earth, unless he is talking only about personal evangelism or missions, someone will object. "Jesus wasn't building a political Kingdom. He was only building His Church. The Church isn't an earthly Kingdom. After all, His Kingdom is not of this world."

It always astounds me when I hear Protestants cite this passage to defend a narrow definition of God's Kingdom. Historically, it was the Roman Catholic Church that equated Kingdom and Church, meaning the Church of Rome. The Protestant Reformation was based on the idea that the institutional Church must be defined much more narrowly than God's all-encompassing Kingdom. The whole idea of "every man a priest"—as Protestant an idea as there is—rests on the assumption that each Christian's service before God is a holy calling, not just the ordained priest's calling. Each Christian serves as a worker in God's Kingdom. Thus, the Kingdom of God is very broad—as broad as Christian service can be.

By defining God's Kingdom very narrowly, Christians are also defining their personal and institutional responsibilities very narrowly. This is precisely the problem: *most Christians fear responsibility.* They fear it so much that they have chosen to define God's Kingdom almost out of earthly existence. In the case of one best-selling Christian author, as we shall see shortly, he has literally defined it out of earthly existence.

What is God's earthly Kingdom? It is the totality of every area of life that has been brought under the healing power of the Gospel. What is the final goal of the Gospel? To subdue every area of life to the glory of God, to bring everything under the dominion of God, with God's redeemed people as His delegated representatives (Genesis 1:26-28). This means that Christians are supposed to extend the limits of God's Kingdom on earth through the preaching of a *comprehensive Gospel.* Each Christian is to discipline himself under God and then go to others and show them what God requires them to do in every area of their lives. The Gospel is as comprehensive as sin is. The Gospel has more power than sin does. Christ has more power than Adam did. Calvary is behind us. Was it not a victory for Christ over Satan in *every* area of Satan's evil-doing? Most Christians today believe that Calvary was not a true historic victory, for sin (they say) will be triumphant until the end of time. They are incorrect.[1]

Christians are told by Jesus to pray, "Thy Kingdom come. Thy will be done in earth as it is in heaven" (Matthew 6:10, KJV). But most Christians today really don't believe that this prayer can or will be answered in history, despite the fact that Jesus asked His people to pray it in history. We should know better: Jesus tells us that our faithful prayers will eventually be answered. "Ask, and it will be given to you; seek, and you will find; knock, and it will be opened to you" (Matthew 7:7). This is why He could tell us in this same Sermon on the Mount: "But seek first the Kingdom of God and His righteousness, and all these things shall be added to you" (Matthew 6:33). *All these things*: this is the final goal of the King-

---

1. Gary North, *Dominion and Common Grace: The Biblical Basis of Progress* (Tyler, Texas: Institute for Christian Economics, 1987).

dom of God in history, toward which we Christians are to labor and pray.

Does this earthly Kingdom include politics? How could it not include politics if it is truly a comprehensive Kingdom? Yet there are millions of Christians today who deny that politics can ever be Christian. Somehow they believe that Christ's offer of salvation is limited in scope—that churches can be healed by grace, families can be healed by grace, businesses can be healed by grace, but "politics is dirty, now and forever more, amen!" They refuse to face the obvious: *politics is a dirty business because Christians have long avoided politics.* Politics is corrupt because Christians have not bothered to search the Scriptures to discover the God-given principles of political action. This lack of concern, this full-time professional Christian apathy, is what *The Changing of the Guard* is designed to overcome.

"Not of This World"

The standard, run-of-the-mill negative Christian response to the Biblical message of Christians' political responsibilities rests on a faulty reading of John 18:36. We need to ask: What did Jesus mean when He said that His Kingdom is not of this world? Jesus was explaining to Pontius Pilate how He could be a king, yet also be standing before Pilate to be judged. Pilate was asking Jesus: "How can you be a king? Where are your defenders? Where is your army?" Pilate believed in the *power religion* of the ancient world.[2] Without earthly armies, he believed, a man cannot be a king. His earth-bound view was echoed over 1,900 years later by the tyrant Joseph Stalin, who is said to have dismissed the authority of the Pope with the comment: "How many divisions does the Pope have?"

Jesus' response to Pilate was clear: the *source* of His kingly authority is not earthly. His Kingdom is not *of* this world. The source of His authority as king is from far *above* this world. His is a *tran-*

---

2. Gary North, *Moses and Pharaoh: Dominion Religion vs. Power Religion* (Tyler, Texas: Institute for Christian Economics, 1985).

scendent Kingdom—distinct from this world—yet it is also *immanent*, meaning that it is present among men in history. His Kingdom reflects His own dual nature: transcendent (perfect God) yet also immanent (perfect man). But there are millions of Christians today who in principle dismiss the doctrine of Christ's perfect humanity in history because they dismiss His Kingdom in history. They spiritualize away His Kingdom, and therefore in principle *they spiritualize away His humanity.* They are the implicit theological defenders of the ancient heresy of docetism—that Christ was God, but not man.

Anyone who argues that politics is permanently corrupt is necessarily arguing that *Christ's salvation cannot heal and restore politics.* Anyone who argues that Christ's salvation cannot heal politics is also implicitly arguing that the humanists have a God-granted right in history to exercise control over politics, since Christians should spend their time bringing the Gospel to those people and institutions that God says can be healed. They ask: "Why waste precious time working on the impossible? Let the humanists do their work while we do ours. Render unto the Caesar the things that are Caesar's." This assumes, of course, that God has in fact given the humanist Caesars of this world permanent possession of political power. Yet this is precisely what the humanists assume, too.

Question: If Caesar gets converted to Christ, should he change his ways? If not, why not? If the answer is "yes," then *there must be God-required ways for Caesar to change to.* In short, is it better to live under Nero or Constantine?

Anyone who argues that the Bible shows us how souls can be saved but not how anything else can be saved has run up the white flag in history to the secular humanists, for if there are no God-required standards of righteousness in politics, then there can be no historical judgment by God over politics. If God has imposed *no law* over something, then He exercises *no jurisdiction* over it. God does not hold anyone responsible for what a person does if He has not placed that person under the specific terms of His covenant. The Bible is quite clear on this point: ". . . sin is not imputed when there is no law" (Romans 5:13b). So, if we argue that men *are* responsible for their evil deeds as politicians, then we must also accept the fact that *there must be God-given standards of righteousness that they have violated.* Finally, if there are God-given standards of political righteousness, then *the Gospel can restore politics to God.* Some Christians may believe that the Gospel will not accomplish this in history, but how can any Christian seriously argue that the gospel cannot accomplish this? Yet millions of them do. They have constructed a social and political worldview on this very assumption.

Warning: if we misinterpret Christ's words, "My Kingdom is not of this world," we will misinterpret the entire New Testament. Inevitable institutional defeat is not what Jesus meant when He said that His Kingdom is not of this world. At the time of His crucifixion, Jesus said that His Kingdom was not then geographically "from here." That is, it did not yet have institutional, visible power on earth. "But *now* My Kingdom is not from here." Nevertheless, His words implied that *at some time in the future*, His Kingdom would indeed possess institutional power. It would then have earthly defenders.

Three centuries later, Christians took over the administration of the remains of the Roman Empire. God's Kingdom by then was visible in a way that Pilate could not have foreseen or foretold.

Conclusion: Christ's Kingdom is not *of* this world as the source of His authority, but it is surely *over* this world in terms of His authority, and it is also *in* this world. If this were not true, then there could be no lawful judgment of this world by God.

The Kingdom on Earth

God's Kingdom possesses earthly manifestations, for Jesus possesses earthly authority. He announced after His resurrection: "All authority has been given to Me in heaven *and on earth.* Go therefore and *make disciples* of all the *nations*, baptizing them in the name of the Father and of the Son and of the Holy Spirit, teaching them *to observe all things that I have commanded you*; and lo, *I am with you always*, even to the end of the age" (Matthew 28:18-20). Discipline the nations, Christ said; this is always the responsibility of

Christians in history. Discipline the nations in terms of my commandments, He said. The Kingdom of God is therefore not an exclusively spiritual affair, nor is it lawless. The Kingdom of God is
not limited to sin-free, flesh-free heaven above.

Rahab, a former pagan harlot, understood the earthly authority of God better than modern Christians do, for she confessed to
the Hebrew spies that "the Lord your God, He is God in heaven
above and on earth beneath" (Joshua 2:11b). This was precisely
what the previous generation of Israelites had not believed. They
believed that the giants in the land of Canaan were too powerful
for them (Numbers 13). They had recommended stoning Joshua
and Caleb for suggesting otherwise (Numbers 14:10).

There are millions of Christians today who have yet to come to
grips with Rahab's confession of faith. They believe that Christ's
authority is exclusively spiritual. (How can anything on earth be
"exclusively spiritual," free of the temptations of money, sex, and
power?) They argue that His Kingdom has only a very limited
manifestation on earth (if any), primarily in the Christian Church
and in Christian families. One best-selling dispensationalist
author has actually written that there will never be *any* earthly
manifestation of the Kingdom of God until after the final judgment. Even during Christ's supposed physical reign on earth during a future earthly millennium, there will be no manifestation of
His Kingdom, for that millennium ends in defeat for the people of
God—a clear defeat for Christ. The God-haters will rebel against
Christ's perfect rule (Revelation 20:8-9). He writes:

> Converging from all over the world to war against Christ and the
> saints at Jerusalem, these rebels will finally have to be banished
> from God's presence forever (Revelation 20:7-10). The millennial
> reign of Christ upon earth, rather than being the kingdom of God,
> will in fact be the final proof of the incorrigible nature of the
> human heart. The true kingdom which "flesh and blood cannot in-
> herit" (1 Corinthians 15:50) pertains to the heart into which Christ
> has been received as Lord and Savior, and will be fully realized
> only in the "new heaven and new earth" (Revelation 21:1).[3]

3. Dave Hunt, *Beyond Seduction: A Return to Biblical Christianity* (Eugene,
Oregon: Harvest House, 1987), pp. 250-51.

This denial of the Kingdom aspects of Christ's personal reign in history is clearly preposterous. I know of no other dispensationalist author who has ever argued such a thing. Why is it preposterous? Because in Isaiah 65, we are told that the New Heaven and New Earth will become manifested *before* the final judgment, for sinners will still live and die among the saints (Isaiah 65:20). We know that sinners will not be operating beyond the day of judgment. Thus, there are preliminary manifestations of the New Heaven and New Earth in history. Second, we are also told concerning Christ and His Kingdom: "Then comes the end, when He delivers the Kingdom to God the Father, when He puts an end to all rule and all authority and power" (1 Corinthians 15:24). Third, we are told that Christ will deliver up His Kingdom to God the Father only after death has been conquered at the final judgment (1 Corinthians 15:25-27). Yet the best-selling spokesman of fundamentalist theology in the mid-1980s rejects all of this in a desperate, futile attempt to internalize every aspect of Christ's Kingdom, in order to persuade his readers that they have no God-assigned Kingdom responsibilities to pursue.

This denial of any aspect of God's Kingdom in history represents *a radical rejection of civic and cultural responsibility*—a rejection which is the psychological (if not theological) culmination of traditional dispensational theology. Even though a handful of dispensational social activists would no doubt reject his conclusions, he does speak for the millions of dispensationalists in the pews who have made him rich and also for most of those in dispensational pulpits. Note also that the leading dispensational institutions have not publicly rejected his spokesmanship of their theological position. Perhaps they are afraid to challenge him, or they may actually agree with him. In either case, this silence in the face of radical cultural retreatism marks the last gasp of traditional dispensationalism; it can no longer be taken seriously as a relevant theological system. The dispensational movement has at last publicly run up the white flag of surrender to the secular humanists.

The divisive issues of eschatology and Biblical law can no longer be contained by the pietists who lead the evangelical com-

tics itself is not central. *The worship of God is central.* The central
issue therefore is this: Which God should mankind worship? The
God of the Bible or a god of man's imagination?

The humanists see the state as man's most powerful institution, and therefore politics is man's most important activity.
Their's is a religion of power, so they make the state the central institution. They make the State their Church.

Because the humanists have made the state into their agency
of earthly salvation, from the ancient Near Eastern empires to the
Greeks to Rome's Empire[5] and to the present, Christians need to
focus on this battlefield, but we must always remember that political battles are important today primarily because *our theological
opponents have chosen to make their first and last stand on the political battlefield.* Had they chosen to fight elsewhere, it would not appear as
though we are hypnotized with the importance of politics. Christian Reconstructionists are not hypnotized by politics; humanists
and piestists are hypnotized by politics. Nevertheless, we are willing to fight the enemy theologically on his chosen ground, for we
are confident that God rules every area of life. He can and will
defeat them in the mountains or on the plains (1 Kings 20:28), in
politics and in education, in family and in business.

What Christians should say in response to humanism's political theology is that *God's Church, as the institution entrusted by God
with His Word and His sacraments, is the central institution of history.*
The Bible teaches that the gates of hell will not stand against the
onslaught of the Church. The Church will be in heaven above and
on the eternal earth after the final judgment. Neither the state nor
the family can legitimately make such a claim. Thus, Christians
must work to reform the Church even more diligently than they
should work to reform politics. If the institutional Church is theologically and morally corrupt, then Christians will lose on the
other battlefields.

Only recently have both humanists and Christians begun to

---

5. R. J. Rushdoony, *The One and the Many: Studies in the Philosophy of Order and
Ultimacy* (Fairfax, Virginia: Thoburn Press, [1971] 1978), chaps. 3-5.

understand that it is God's institutional Church that must be subdued by humanists, or else the effects of Christ's saving Gospel will subdue them. The humanists use political power to subdue the Church, while the Church is supposed to use the Gospel to subdue the humanists.

Yet it is sadly the case that *the vast majority of today's Bible-believing Christians agree with the humanists with respect to the centrality of politics in all social reform.* This faith in politics as the primary means of social transformation is the great myth of our era, and most fundamentalists and evangelicals have adopted it. Traditional fundamentalists and traditional humanists agree that the primary manifestation of earthly sovereignty is political. Traditional fundamentalists flee politics as inherently evil, since they recognize people cannot be saved by politics. Traditional humanists seek political power because they believe that the only possible salvation society can enjoy must come through politics. Neither group acknowledges that politics is not central in programs of cultural reform.

Christian Reconstructionists call Christians into the political arena, *and also into all other cultural arenas*, in the name of Christ. Christian pietists resent this. They resent the idea that they are responsible for politics or anything else outside the local Church. This is why pietist critics of dominion theology again and again erroneously argue that the heart of dominion theology is the capture of the civil government by Christians. Over and over they warn against this "exclusive" concern of the Christian Reconstructionists (the social theorists of the dominion theology movement). The fact is, it is the theology of Christian Reconstructionism that alone in our day offers a self-consciously Biblical rejection of humanism's statist social theory. Christian Reconstructionists categorically *deny* that politics is central to social change. The reformation of the Church is central; every other positive social change will flow from this one.

The battle with humanism is intensifying, for a growing number of traditional fundamentalists are abandoning the older hostility to social and political involvement. As yet, very few

Christians possess a consistent worldview that informs them concerning why they have left the older retreatist outlook. A growing minority of Christians are outraged with abortion, humanism in the public schools, pornography, and similar issues that have begun to overcome the traditional pietistic theologies of noninvolvement. They recognize that their public protests against public evil are considered strange and even dangerous by pietists in their churches — the majority of members. They have waited in vain for any Bible-believing seminary to come out forthrightly against abortion and begin to train students in how to shut down an abortion clinic. They have begun to perceive that there are deep theological reasons why these seminaries do not assign a book like Joseph Scheidler's *Closed: 99 Ways to Stop Abortion* (Crossway, 1985). They have begun to recognize the grim reality: these institutions have rejected the New Testament validity of Old Testament law. They have no specific, socially relevant, Bible-based answers to the question: By what standard? Seminary faculty members do not believe that Christians are going to be victorious in history, and so they are uninterested in exploring the Biblical basis of social reform. Therefore, a growing minority of Christian activists have at last begun to turn to the long-abandoned theology that was the foundation of the Christian West until the late nineteenth century: *dominion theology.* They have begun a search for Biblical blueprints.

The consistent secular humanist and the consistent Christian can agree on these two things: first, there is an earth, and second, somebody owns it and, therefore, somebody has to control it. The question is, which God owns it and controls it? Another question is: Who *speaks* in the name of this God?

The side that wins this theological war in the public arena will provide the cultural answers for many generations. So far, Christians have been losing this war. I believe that this is going to change in the near future. When it does, there will be a revolution in the thinking of millions of Christians. They are going to abandon the traditional eschatologies of earthly defeat.

Revolutions and Political Theory

Sheldon Wolin taught for many years at the Berkeley campus of the University of California. Wolin was one of the earliest of the professors at Berkeley to support publicly the aims of the student revolution of the late 1960s, and he was one of the most prestigious professors to do so. He is also the author of an influential textbook in political philosophy, which is far more than a textbook. It is a brilliant humanist defense of political participation as something remarkably close institutionally and psychologically to the sacrament of the Lord's Supper. In short, he regards politics as something bordering on being a secular substitute for worship.

Early in his book, he makes a very important observation. I believe the phenomena described by this observation will become increasingly important to Christians over the next two decades. In fact, I believed in the truth of this observation so much that I decided to publish *The Changing of the Guard*. Wolin writes:

> . . . most of the great statements of political philosophy have been put forward in times of crisis; that is, when political phenomena are less effectively integrated by institutional forms. Institutional breakdown releases phenomena, so to speak, causing political behavior and events to take on something of a random quality, and destroying customary meanings that had been part of the old political world.[6]

This is fancy academic language for a simple idea: when things blow up politically, new people pick up the pieces, and then other bright new people start rethinking the proper arrangement of the theoretical puzzle of politics and government. The theoretical puzzle gets put back together very differently, just as the various institutional puzzles get put back together differently, and new words and concepts are developed that help justify (and even actively promote) the new political arrangements.

In short, some people win, and others lose. Most people don't

---

6. Sheldon Wolin, *Politics and Vision: Continuity and Innovation in Western Political Thought* (Boston: Little, Brown, 1960), p. 8.

care one way or the other, if they are left alone—if they are *allowed*
to be left alone. But in the revolutionary political changes of the
last two centuries, almost nobody has been left alone. Revolutionary humanists, unlike most Christians today, have long recognized that the war between humanism and Christianity is total,
and it therefore involves everyone and everything. Nobody is
allowed to be left alone. It is this fact that Christians in the United
States have only begun to recognize since 1980: *the humanist state is
not going to leave Christians alone.* Furthermore, it never intended to
leave them alone; and this disturbing realization on the part of
Christians is part of the faint signs of a coming political transformation. As Christians begin to rethink their situation, something
unique is taking place in their thinking. For one thing, you are
reading this book. Would you have read it five or ten years ago,
had it been available?

Wolin has argued that political revolutions create revolutions
in political theory. Since 1965, the West has been experiencing the
preliminary shocks of a looming political earthquake. At the University of Houston in the early 1970s, George Grant became
fascinated with the teachings of Sheldon Wolin. He studied under
one of Wolin's former students. Oddly enough, a dozen years earlier I too had studied political thought under another of Wolin's
former graduate students. Grant understands the potentially revolutionary nature of the next dozen or so years. His book reflects
this awareness.

George Grant brought some unique qualifications to this writing
project. Besides having pastored a Church for nearly a decade in
Houston, Texas, he is the author of several ground-breaking books
on current social issues and theology. He is the president of HELP
Services, a charitable relief organization that has been profiled in
the national media including the *Wall Street Journal*, ABC's *Nightline*,
and CBN's *700 Club*. He also serves as the host of the nationally
syndicated radio program, "Christian Worldview," as the president
of a Crisis Pregnancy Center, and as the director of LifeNet, a
coalition of pro-life organizations in the Texas-Gulf Coast region.

Grant believes that the coming disruptions of the world economy and the international political order will provide an unprecedented opportunity for Christians to become dominant in politics.

The question is: Will they make good use of this opportunity?

God and Government

Politics is the means of establishing and controlling civil government. It is one of the great heresies of our era that most people believe that civil government is "government," and that other lawful, God-ordained governments are something less than government. It is this monopolizing of the concept of government by the state that is at the heart of the loss of liberty in our day. (See Gary DeMar's book in the Biblical Blueprints Series, *Ruler of the Nations*.)

Conservative sociologist and historian Robert Nisbet has written in his classic book, *The Quest for Community* (1952), that "The argument of this book is that the single most decisive influence upon Western social organization has been the rise and development of the centralized territorial State."[7] He goes on to say, "Unlike either kinship or capitalism, the State has become, in the contemporary world, the supreme allegiance of men and, in most recent times, the greatest refuge from the insecurities of and frustrations of other spheres of life. . . . [T]he State has risen as the dominant institutional force in our society and the most evocative symbol of cultural unity and purpose."[8] He is correct when he says that this modern faith in the State as the supreme manifestation of man's unity, purpose, and power "makes control of the State the greatest single goal, or prize, in modern struggles for power."[9]

It is this struggle for control over the state that is the equivalent of medieval man's quest for salvation. What Prof. Wolin wishes to accelerate—the substitution of political participation for religious participation—his former faculty colleague at Berkeley,

---

7. Nisbet, *The Quest for Community* (New York: Oxford University Press, 1952), p. 98.
8. *Ibid.*, p. 99.
9. *Ibid.*, p. 103.

The Changing of the Guard

Robert Nisbet, wishes to reverse. What Wolin says is the great evil of modern political philosophy—the separation of state and society[10]—Prof. Nisbet says has not gone far enough, and therefore he wants to reaffirm that very separation.[11] Society is far more than the state; it is a complex of lawful institutions—families, churches, businesses, and many voluntary associations and memberships. A denial of the distinction between society and state is, Nisbet argues, the first step toward totalitarianism.

The authors who are involved in this Biblical Blueprints Series are convinced that we are now moving into such a period in history—not just U.S. history, but world history. Every inhabited continent is being plowed up institutionally and religiously by God. This process is unquestionably worldwide in scope. Telecommunications now link the whole world, and so does the New York Stock Exchange. For the first time in human history, the whole world is operating with the same science, technology, and mathematics. It is also struggling with the same fundamental philosophical questions. The whole world is experiencing the same breakdown in covenant-breaking man's ability to understand and govern His world. *God is plowing it up.*

We are rapidly approaching the year 2000, an apocalyptic sounding year if there ever was one. The sense of urgency will only increase from this point forward.

When we hear the word "revolution," we usually think politics and bombs. But revolutions don't spring up full grown overnight. They don't take place in historical vacuums. They take a lot of planning. *Revolutions are always preceded by major shifts in people's thinking, especially the thinking of the intellectual elite.* This is taking place now. The humanist intellectual elite is visibly in philosophical retreat. World leaders have lost confidence in the existing liberal worldview. There are no more self-attesting truths in the world of humanism any longer, except one: that the God of the Bible isn't possible.

10. Wolin, *Politics and Vision*, ch. 10.
11. Nisbet, *Quest for Community*, ch. 5.

Revival

Christians are praying for a worldwide revival. If such a revival comes, that last humanist truth will be abandoned. People will believe that the God of the Bible is not only possible, He has in fact entered into their lives personally. But when this revolutionary shift of faith comes, what will Christians recommend in place of today's collapsing humanist culture? That's what these Biblical blueprints are all about: building a new world with God's permanent moral and institutional blueprints.

We need to begin to train ourselves to make the transition in every area of life. This includes politics. As *The Changing of the Guard* shows, God has given His people major political responsibilities that they have neglected for at least seventy years and more like a century.[12] Christians are being challenged by God to reclaim the political realm for Jesus Christ. We must publicly declare the crown rights of King Jesus.

Christians today have a golden opportunity—an opportunity that doesn't come even as often as once in a lifetime. It comes about once every 250 years. The last time it came for Christians was during the American Revolution era (1776-1789). The revolutionary humanists who created and ran the French Revolution (1789-95) created a satanic alternative, one which is with us still in the demonic empire of communism.

A showdown is coming in time and on earth: Christ vs. Satan, Christianity vs. humanism, the dominion religion vs. the power religion. You are being called to take up a position of responsibility on the side of Christ. One aspect of this responsibility is to render Biblical political judgments. This book will help to show you why this is your responsibility and what you can do about it.

It is time to begin to prepare ourselves for an unprecedented revival. It is time to prepare ourselves for a *changing of the guard*—in every area of life, all over the world. Our preparation must help

---

12. Douglas Frank, *Less Than Conquerors: How Evangelicals Entered the Twentieth Century* (Grand Rapids, Michigan: Eerdmans, 1986).

us to answer the hoped-for question of God-fearing new converts to Christ: "I'm saved; what now?"

The Covenant Structure

To get the right answers, we need first to ask the right questions. For a long, long time, Christians and Jews have had the right questions right under their noses, but no one paid any attention. The questions concerning lawful government are organized in the Bible around a single theme: *the covenant.*

Most Christians and Jews have heard the word "covenant." They regard themselves (and occasionally even each other) as covenant people. They are taught from their youth about God's covenant with Israel and how this covenant extends (or doesn't) to the Christian church. Everyone talks about the covenant, but until late 1985, nobody did anything about it.

Not in 3,400 years of (non-inspired) Bible commentaries.

Am I exaggerating? Test me. Go to a Christian or a Jew and ask him to outline the basic features of the Biblical covenant. He will not be able to do it rapidly or even believably. Ask two Jews or two Christians who talk about the covenant, and compare the answers. The answers will not fit very well.

For over four centuries, Calvinist theologians have talked about the covenant. They are even known as *covenant theologians.* The Puritans of the 1600s wrote seemingly endless numbers of books about the covenant. The problem is, nobody has ever been able to come up with "the" covenant model in the writings of Calvin, let alone all his followers. The Calvinists have hung their theological hats on the covenant, yet they have never put down on paper precisely what it is, what it involves, and how it works — in the Bible or in church history.

Then, in late 1985, Pastor Ray Sutton made an astounding discovery. He was thinking about Biblical symbols, and he struggled with the question of two New Testament covenant symbols, baptism and communion. This in turn raised the question of the Old Testament's covenant symbols, circumcision and passover. What do these symbols have in common? Obviously, the covenant. But what, precisely, is the covenant? Is it the same in both Testaments (Covenants)?

He began rereading some books by Calvinist theologian Meredith G. Kline. In several books (really, collections of essays), Kline mentioned the structure of the Book of Deuteronomy. He argued that Deuteronomy's structure in fact parallels the ancient pagan world's special documents that are known as the suzerain (king-vassal) treaties.

That triggered something in Sutton's mind. Kline discusses the outline of these treaties in several places. In some places, he says they have five sections; in other places, he indicates that they may have had six or even seven. It was all somewhat vague. So Sutton sat down with Deuteronomy to see what the structure is. He found five parts.

Then he looked at other books of the Bible that are known to be divided into five parts: Psalms and Matthew. He believes that he found the same structure. Then he went to other books, including some Pauline epistles. He found it there, too. When he discussed his findings in a Wednesday evening Bible study, David Chilton instantly recognized the same structure in the Book of Revelation. He had been working sporadically on a commentary on Revelation for over three years, and he had it divided into four parts. Sutton and Chilton discussed the covenant structure off and on for several weeks. Chilton then went to his computer and shifted around the manuscript's sections electronically. The results of his restructuring can be read in his marvelous commentary on the Book of Revelation, *The Days of Vengeance* (Dominion Press, 1987).

Here, then, is the five-point structure of the Biblical covenant, as developed by Sutton in his excellent book, *That You May Prosper: Dominion By Covenant* (Institute for Christian Economics, 1987).

1. The transcendence and presence of God
2. Hierarchy/authority
3. Biblical law/dominion
4. Judgment/sanctions: blessings and cursings
5. Inheritance/continuity

Simple, isn't it? Yet it has implications beyond your wildest imagination. Here is the key that unlocks the structure of human government. Here is the structure that Christians can use to analyze church, state, family, and numerous other non-covenantal but contractual institutions.

It can be used to unlock the long-debated structure of the Ten Commandments: 1-5, with a parallel 6-10. I spotted this almost as soon as Sutton described his discovery to me, just as I was finishing my economic commentary on the Ten Commandments, *The Sinai Strategy* (Institute for Christian Economics, 1986), which I outlined in the Preface. It can also be used to make sense out of some of the basic concepts of economics, as I show in my book in the Biblical Blueprints Series, *Inherit the Earth* (1987). In fact, once you begin to work with this model, it becomes difficult not to see it everywhere you look. This means that this model is either very powerful or very hypnotizing.

Where the intellectual payoff really gets high is in the study of government. Gary DeMar did not deliberately structure his first draft of *Ruler of the Nations* (1987) around Deuteronomy's five-point covenant model. Nevertheless, as I read it, I recognized the five points. I simply moved his chapters around. He had already covered the basic topics of government that the five-point model reveals: in two sets of five chapters. Once again, we see the power of this covenant model. Without deliberately imitating it, DeMar asked the questions raised by the covenant model. He just didn't originally ask them in the covenant model's order. I had almost the identical experience in editing George Grant's book.

Let us consider the five simple questions that this model raises for those studying the various institutions of government.

1. Who's in charge here?
2. To whom do I report?
3. What are the rules?
4. What happens to me if I obey (disobey)?
5. Does this outfit have a future?

As you read *The Changing of the Guard*, you will see just how important the covenant structure is as a way to understand what politics is all about and what the Christian's responsibility is in this important area of human life. *The Changing of the Guard* discusses numerous political aspects of God's Kingdom. Understand, however, that it is not the only book in the Biblical Blueprints Series. The series is an entire shelf of books dealing with the requirements that God has set forth to His people concerning their earthly responsibilities for constructing His Kingdom. Christians are required by God to become active in building God's visible Kingdom. Unfortunately, most people today think "politics" when they hear the word "activism." Such a conclusion is incorrect. This is the error of the modern humanist as well as the ancient pagan; it should not be the error of the Christian.

Then Jesus came and spoke to them, saying, "All authority has been given to Me in heaven and on earth. Go therefore and make disciples of all the nations, baptizing them in the name of the Father and of the Son and the Holy Spirit, teaching them to observe all things that I have commanded you; and lo, I am with you always, even to the end of the age.

Matthew 28:18-20

Part I
BLUEPRINTS

We were available, but unable.

Still, we've made a difference. We've became a force to be reckoned with.

In less than a decade, we have been transformed from cultural irrelevance and epistemological unconsciousness into a genuine threat to the liberal humanist establishment. We've rediscovered the world and we've rediscovered the fact that "righteousness exalts a nation, but sin is a reproach to any people" (Proverbs 14:34).

For that we might issue forth with great rejoicing.

At long last, Christians have heard and heeded Christ's call to go to the world with redemption and life (John 17:15-18).

Call out the brass bands. Strike up the hallelujahs.

But before we get too carried away, let's pause to consider just what is going on here. We must be careful. A balance must be forged. Though it is criminal to allow the Gospel to become culturally and politically *irrelevant*, it is *equally* criminal to allow the Gospel to become *centered* in cultural and political concerns. We must not twist the message of the Scriptures into *either* an "Escapist Gospel" *or* a "Social Gospel." We must not allow the Church to be a pawn of *either* liberal humanism *or* conservative humanism. *Both* extremes are a perversion of the truth.

The Bible tells us that this world "lies in the power of the evil one" (1 John 5:19), but at the same time, it tells us that God *loves* the world and He sent His Son not to condemn it, but to *save* it (John 3:16-17).

The Bible tells us that, while God *does* love the world (Ephesians 2:4), believers must *not* love it (1 John 2:15); in fact, anyone who is a friend of the world is an enemy of God (James 4:14).

The Bible tells us that the world came into existence by Christ (John 1:3; Colossians 1:16) and that He alone sustains and maintains it (Colossians 1:17; Hebrews 1:3). But at the same time, He does not intercede on its behalf (John 17:9).

The Bible tells us that the world is a rich field for the sowing of the Word (Matthew 13:36-38). But at the same time, it hates the sower, Christ, because He testifies that its deeds are evil (John 7:7).

A number of Christians in America have indeed rediscovered

the world, but we have hardly settled the issue of what we are to *do* now that the discovery has been made.

This book is an attempt to explore that issue. It is not a book of anecdotes and stories about early America or Reagan's America; it is an investigation into the *Biblical* teachings on the world and the world's institutions. It is not a handbook of political intrigue. It is an exposition and application of the Scriptural principles of civil action.

Should Christians be involved in politics? If so, how should we act? What should we do? How far should we go? What should be our agenda?

These are the questions that this manuscript will attempt to answer. They are *practical* questions. And the Bible offers *practical* answers. Hopefully, *The Changing of the Guard* will take those *practical* questions and *practical* answers and illumine them — *practically.*

Part I explores ten basic principles of the Biblical blueprint for political action. It probes the issues of our day through the perspective of Scripture. Lots and lots of Bible passages are marshalled to the task — as they should be.

"All Scripture is given by inspiration of God, and is profitable for doctrine, for reproof, for correction, for instruction in righteousness, that the man of God may be complete, thoroughly equipped for every good work" (2 Timothy 3:16-17). Thus to attempt to reform the world without taking heed to the clear instruction of the Bible is utter foolishness (Romans 1:18-23). It is to invite inadequacy and incompetency (Deuteronomy 28:15). All such attempts are doomed to frustration and failure (Deuteronomy 30:15-20). Humanism *can't* work — whether conservative or liberal — because humanism is out of touch with reality (Ephesians 5:6). It is fraught with fantasy (Colossians 2:8). Only the Bible can tell us of things as they *really* are (Psalm 19:7-11). Only the Bible faces reality squarely, practically, completely, and honestly (Deuteronomy 30:11-14). Thus, only the Bible can provide genuine solutions to the problems that plague mankind.

Once a clear and principled picture has been drawn of the Bible's blueprint for politics, then — and only then — can specific political actions be recommended (Deuteronomy 15:4-8). Only then can strategies be outlined, tactics designed, and programs initiated (Joshua 1:8).

That is where Part II comes in. There specific steps of action are outlined for churches, families, and individuals who, having rediscovered the world, wish to change it — *Biblically*.

Christian philosopher Cornelius Van Til has stated, "The Bible is authoritative on everything of which it speaks. And it speaks of everything." Even of such "mundane" matters as political action. Thus, to evoke Scripture's blueprint for our cosmopolitan culture's complex dilemmas is not some naive resurrection of musty, dusty archaisms. "More than that, blessed are those who hear the Word of God, and keep it" (Luke 11:28). For, "the Scripture cannot be broken" (John 10:35).

I. Transcendence/Presence

1

THE EARTH IS THE LORD'S

All this came upon King Nebuchadnezzar. At the end of the twelve months he was walking about the royal palace of Babylon. The king spoke, saying, "Is not this great Babylon, that I have built for a royal dwelling by my mighty power and for the honor of majesty?"

While the word was still in the king's mouth, a voice fell from heaven: "King Nebuchadnezzar, to you it is spoken: the kingdom has departed from you! And they shall drive you from men, and your dwelling shall be with the beasts of the field. They shall make you eat grass like oxen; and seven times shall pass over you, until you know that the Most High rules in the kingdom of men, and gives it to whomever He chooses" (Daniel 4:28-32).

He was the greatest king of the ancient world. His reign was resplendent with glory, honor, and power. The city that he built was utterly magnificent, unrivaled in its scope and vision. The empire that he assembled was mythically proportioned, unrivaled in its strength and valor. The reputation that he forged was universally terrifying, unrivaled in its supremacy and vastness. And yet, Nebuchadnezzar was still but a man.

He *thought* he was something more. He imagined for himself a majesty that transcended that of all other men. He reveled in the storehouse of his great pride. He boasted of his invincibility.

And so, God humbled him. He decreed that Nebuchadnezzar would be reminded of the frailty of human flesh. He decreed that the great king would be forced to acknowledge a King greater still.

Immediately the word concerning Nebuchadnezzar was fulfilled; and he was driven away from mankind and began eating grass like cattle, and his body was drenched with the dew of heaven, until his hair grew like eagles' feathers, and his nails like birds' claws (Daniel 4:33).

The complete demise of Nebuchadnezzar was a vivid demonstration to all the citizens of Babylon that *God alone* is sovereign and all-mighty (Revelation 17:14), that *God alone* is exalted and praised (Psalm 148:13), that *God alone* is the possessor of all greatness, power, glory, and majesty in heaven and on earth (1 Chronicles 29:11).

The lesson was not lost on the king or his subjects.

But at the end of that period, I, Nebuchadnezzar, raised my eyes toward heaven, and my reason returned to me, and I blessed the Most High and praised and honored Him who lives forever. For His dominion is an everlasting dominion; and His kingdom endures from generation to generation. And all the inhabitants of the earth are counted as nothing, but He does according to His will in the host of heaven and among the inhabitants of the earth. And no one can ward off his hand or say to him: "What hast Thou done?"

At that time my reason returned to me. And my majesty and splendor were restored to me for the glory of my kingdom, and my counselors and my nobles began seeking me out; so I was reestablished in my sovereignty, and surpassing greatness was added to me. Now I, Nebuchadnezzar praise, exalt, and honor the King of heaven, for all His works are true and His ways just, and He is able to humble those who walk in pride (Daniel 4:34-37).

Nebuchadnezzar learned the most central truth in all the cosmos: *God rules* (Psalm 103:19). He learned that God and God alone is supreme (Isaiah 40:17-18), that God is the "King of kings and Lord of lords" (1 Timothy 6·15). God rules because He is the *creator* and the *owner* of all things:

The Lord God Most High is the possessor of heaven and earth (Genesis 14:22).

Behold, to the Lord your God belong heaven and the highest heavens, the earth and all that is in it (Deuteronomy 10:14).

The earth is the Lord's and all it contains, the world, and those who dwell in it. For He has founded it upon the seas, and established it upon the rivers (Psalm 24:1-2).

God Rules

Nebuchadnezzar had to learn the hard way that the whole universe is a *theocracy* (theos = God, kratos = rules). It is a theocracy *now*. God's rule is not something we must wait for. It is a reality right this very moment. "Hallelujah! For the Lord our God, the Almighty, reigns" (Revelation 19:6).

The Bible is absolutely clear on this point. There is nothing in heaven above or on earth below that escapes His jurisdiction. *God rules*.

God rules the forces of creation:

I know that the Lord is great, and that our Lord is above all gods. Whatever the Lord pleases, He does, in heaven and in earth, in the seas and in all deeps. He causes the vapors to ascend from the ends of the earth; who makes lightnings for the rain; who brings forth the wind from His treasuries (Psalm 135:5-7).

He sends forth His command to the earth; His word runs very swiftly. He gives snow like wool; He scatters the frost like ashes. He casts forth His ice as fragments; Who can stand before His cold? He sends forth His Word and melts them; He causes His wind to blow and the waters to flow (Psalm 147:15-18).

For from Him and through Him and to Him are all things (Romans 11:36).

The Lord has made everything for His own purpose (Proverbs 16:4).

God rules the course of history:

He works all things after the counsel of His own will (Ephesians 1:11).

Remember the former things long past, for I am God, and there is no other; I am God, and there is no one like Me, declaring and that there will be no end to the increase of His government or of peace (Isaiah 9:7). It freely confesses what Nebuchadnezzar was forced to admit: "His dominion is an everlasting dominion, and His kingdom endures from generation to generation" (Daniel 4:34). Christian political action is nothing more and nothing less than the declaration: "Jesus is Lord"— *the most basic of all Christian declarations* (Romans 10:9).

For a Christian to ignore the realm of politics is to ignore *the regency of Jesus Christ*. It is to commit the foolish *error* of Nebuchadnezzar and thus to risk the open *shame* of Nebuchadnezzar.

Sadly, most twentieth century evangelical Christians have followed in that Babylonian king's ignoble footsteps. We have ignored the fact that Christ bears the ensigns of the theocracy: a *crown* of glory and honor (Hebrews 2:9), a *sword* of truth and justice (Revelation 1:16; 2:16), a *scepter* of righteousness and authority (Hebrews 1:8), a *crest* of promise and consolation (Revelation 5:5), a *name* of prerogative and transcendence (Philippians 2:9-10), and a *title deed* of absoluteness and finality (Matthew 11:29). We have acted as if the Lordship of Christ were not the least bit real. We have acted like Nebuchadnezzar. As a result, we have, like Nebuchadnezzar, suffered utter humiliation. The enemies of the Gospel scoff and ridicule. They persecute and antagonize. They run roughshod over the weak and helpless. They pollute the land with abomination and desecration. And all the while, we are scuttled off to pasture like so many bovine indigents (Daniel 4:33). All for the lack of a simple declaration that Christ is the Lord over the totality of life—that *God rules*.

Of course, Nebuchadnezzar learned *his* lesson. His humiliation convinced him beyond any shadow of a doubt that it is God who "removes kings and establishes kings" (Daniel 2:21); it is God who appoints over the land whomsoever He will (Daniel 5:21); it is God who *rules* on earth as He does in heaven (Psalm 110:1-3). Nebuchadnezzar learned his lesson and changed his heart *and* his politics. It remains to be seen if *we* will learn *our lesson*. It remains to be seen if we will translate *our humiliation* into a confession of Christ's exaltation to the throne of authority and rule.

The American Legacy

In this regard it would stand us in good stead to recall our heritage. The founders and early leaders of the American republic had no trouble whatsoever acknowledging the theocracy of heaven and earth. Their political actions were thoroughly rooted in the realization that God rules.

George Washington (who was actually our *eighth* president, but the first under the *present* constitution) added the pledge, "So help me, God," to his inauguration oath, and then stooped to kiss the Bible as an affirmation of his submission to the rule of God. He later asserted, "It is impossible to rightly govern the world without God and the Bible."

John Adams, the second president under the present constitution, made no secret of the fact that he studied the Bible often and with diligence in order to discern the proper administration of God's rule. He said, "Our constitution was made only for a moral and religious people . . . so great is my veneration of the Bible that the earlier my children begin to read it, the more confident will be my hope that they will prove useful citizens of their country and respectful members of society."

Thomas Jefferson, primary author of the Declaration of Independence and the third president, was also quite forthright in his acknowledgement of universal theocracy. He said, "The Bible is the cornerstone of liberty . . . students' perusal of the sacred volume will make us better citizens, better fathers, and better husbands."

Benjamin Franklin, the patriarch of the fledgling American republic, said, "A nation of well informed men who have been taught to know the price of the rights which God has given them, cannot be enslaved."

William Penn, founder and governor of the Pennsylvania colony, stated the case plainly when he said, "If we will not be governed by God, then we will be ruled by tyrants."

Andrew Jackson, the country's seventh president, read the Bible daily in deference to God's immutable reign, and referred to it as "the Rock on which our republic rests."

throned on high. We need only to *recognize* His Lordship in word and in deed.

Christian political action then is simply submitting to the authority of God in every sphere of life through the application of His Word in every institution in life. It is a confession that "the earth is the Lord's and everything in it, the world and all who live in it" (Psalm 24:1).

Nebuchadnezzar had to learn the hard way that God will not tolerate any other perspective. But there is no need for us to share in his shame and humiliation.

Our republic was built on an understanding of God's rule and all the liberties we enjoy can be traced directly to the foundation that that understanding laid.

If we are to have any hope of preserving our civilization from the ravages of sin and destruction, we must once again affirm the Lordship of Christ. We must root our political activity in the rule and reign of God Almighty.

Summary

Nebuchadnezzar, the greatest of all the ancient kings, was deposed by God Himself to demonstrate that He alone is the Most High Ruler of all things.

God, in fact, sovereignly rules the *entire* cosmos: the forces of creation, the course of history, the hearts and minds and ways of men, and the nations of the earth.

Christian political action is therefore an acknowledgement of the theocracy of heaven and earth. It is the simple declaration that "Jesus is Lord."

This declaration of Christ's authority became the basis of the American political system.

And it must be the basis of our political efforts as we struggle against a Nebuchadnezzar-like messianic state.

We must once again sound the clarion call of liberty and justice: "Our God reigns."

2

RENDER UNTO HIM

Then they sent to Him some of the Pharisees and the Herodians, to catch Him in His words. When they had come, they said to Him, "Teacher, we know that You are true, and care about no one; for You do not regard the person of men, but teach the way of God in truth. Is it lawful to pay taxes to Caesar, or not? Shall we pay, or shall we not pay?" But He, knowing their hypocrisy, said to them, "Why do you test me? Bring me a denarius that I may see it." So they brought it. And He said to them, "Whose image and inscription is this?" And they said to Him, "Caesar's." Then Jesus answered and said to them, "Render to Caesar the things that are Caesar's, and to God the things that are God's." And they marveled at Him (Mark 12:13-17).

The Pharisees and Herodians came to trap Jesus. Instead, the Master trapped *them*.

First, Jesus embarrassed them. He demonstrated that *they* had *already* recognized and legitimized Roman authority by virtue of the fact that they had a denarius in their possession. They had *already* accepted the *fact* of Roman rule. They were using Rome's coins! Thus, their question was exposed as insincere and hypocritical.

Second, Jesus rebuked them. He not only affirmed the legitimacy of the established powers and the moral obligation of rendering them their due, He also put those powers in perspective saying, "Render unto God the things that are God's" (Luke 20:25).

The Pharisees and Herodians knew precisely what Jesus

17

God and the state. In truth, everything that the state is, every authority that it wields, every jurisdiction that it holds, and every issue that it governs has been delegated to it by God. Rulers, magistrates, and judges are "servants" (Romans 13:6) and "ministers" (Romans 13:4) accountable to God.

Thus, like the family and the Church, the state is to be considered sacred: ruled by God, ordered by His Word, and entrusted to men as a divine arena for the proving of righteousness. And like the family and the Church, the state is to be considered by faithful Christians to be a legitimate, and indeed, an essential area of calling and ministry. It is as honorable and holy a pursuit as is fatherhood or evangelism or the pastorate.

When was the last time you heard of someone submitting to a call into the ministry—the ministry of political action?

There can be no doubt that God called *Joseph* into such a ministry (Genesis 41:39-41). Though the path to power was difficult, there was never any question in his mind that God had chosen him to govern (Genesis 37:5-10) in order to bring glory to God (Genesis 50:20) and to save his people (Genesis 45:1).

There can be no doubt that God also called *Gideon* into such a ministry (Judges 6:11-14). He was a simple farmer (Judges 6:11). But he was obedient to God's call (Judges 6:33-35) and took seriously his holy occupation (Judges 7:2-9). As a result, God delivered the nation (Judges 7:19-25).

There can be no doubt that God also called *Deborah* into the ministry of political action (Judges 5:1-7). She was a prophetess (Judges 4:4) renowned throughout the land for her anointing and judgment (Judges 4:5). Had it not been for her courageous leadership, the land would have been sorely oppressed and the enemies of God would have triumphed (Judges 4:6-24).

There can be no doubt that God called *Samuel* into the ministry of political action as well (1 Samuel 3:1-19). He had been set aside for service to the Lord from birth (1 Samuel 1:27-28) and answered the call early to judge the civil affairs of the nation (1 Samuel 7:15-17).

There can be no doubt that God also called *David* into the

ministry of political action (1 Samuel 16:1-13). Though he was the youngest child in a family of poor shepherds (1 Samuel 16:11) and despised by his own brethren (1 Samuel 17:28), God raised him up to be the greatest of Israel's many kings (2 Samuel 2:4), a man after God's heart (1 Samuel 16:7).

There can be no doubt that God also called *Josiah* into the ministry of political action (2 Kings 22:1). As the leader of his nation, he restored the Word of God to its rightful place (2 Kings 23:3-15). He rid the land of idolatry and debauchery (2 Kings 23:19-24), and he made the name of the Lord great, serving Him with all his heart and soul and might (2 Kings 23:25).

There can be no doubt that God also called *Nehemiah* into the ministry of political action (Nehemiah 1:1-11). He utilized his position of authority to remove the shame of his people (Nehemiah 2:1-20), to restore them to their proper stature (Nehemiah 4:1-23), and to reestablish civil integrity in the land (Nehemiah 13:4-28).

There can be no doubt that God called *Daniel* into that ministry as well (Daniel 1:2-20). From his youth, God endowed him with great wisdom, deep understanding, discerning knowledge, and an ability for governmental service (Daniel 1:4). He studied diligently (Daniel 1:18) and demonstrated faithfulness (Daniel 1:20), so that the cause of the Kingdom and the name of the Lord were exalted throughout the land (Daniel 4:1-3).

Each of these heroes of the faith understood clearly that there was no wall of separation between God and the state. They knew that God had ordained and established civil government just as surely as He had the family and the Church. So they looked upon political action as a holy calling, a ministry, a sacred service before God.

They knew that:

> When it goes well with the righteous, the city rejoices, and when the wicked perish, there is glad shouting. By the blessing of the upright a city is exalted, but by the mouth of the wicked it is torn down (Proverbs 11:10-11).

And that:

> Righteousness exalts a nation, but sin is a disgrace to any people (Proverbs 14:34).

Pharisees and Herodians

The Pharisees in ancient Israel were a party of religious fundamentalists. The Herodians were a party of political statists. The Pharisees' name literally meant "the separatists," so concerned were they with remaining unstained by the world. The Herodians' name implied a close connection with one of the most worldly, vile, and xenophobic men in all history. The Pharisees withdrew from occupations of power and influence in order to focus on "spiritual things." The Herodians grasped for such occupations with undeterred zeal in order to focus on "earthly things."

And yet these two parties, so diametrically opposed in every other way, became partners by their opposition to Jesus (Mark 3:6; 12:13; Matthew 22:16). Paganism makes for strange bedfellows: the Pharasaic sons of Jacob became the unwitting political accomplices of the Herodian sons of Esau (Mark 3:8).

The Pharisees opposed Jesus because they felt He had polluted the spiritual realm with such earthly cares as caring for the poor. The Herodians opposed Jesus because they felt He had polluted the earthly realm with spiritual cares, such as bringing every area of life publicly under God's rule.

So the two parties—the pietistic escapists and the materialistic autonomists—became co-belligerants. They joined forces to assert a separation between God and state.

Interestingly, after nearly two millennia, the two parties still exist. And they are still joined together in opposition to the Gospel of Christ.

The party of the Pharisees is well represented by the evangelical Church, of all things. We have abandoned our God-ordained commission to be salt and light (Matthew 5:13-16). We have abandoned our dominion mandate (Genesis 1:28) and our commission to disciple the nations (Matthew 28:19-20). Instead, we have emphasized a Pharisaic or Separatist view of piety wherein a sharp division is made between the "spiritual" and the "material." Since we, like the Pharisees before us, consider the "spiritual" realm to be superior to the "material," all things physical, all things temporal, all things earthly are spurned. Political action is thus left in the lands of evil-doers. Although the Bible asserts that we are to think hard about the nature of Christian civilization (1 Peter 1:13), to try to develop Biblical alternatives to humanistic society (Matthew 18:15-20), and to prophesy Biblically to the cultural problems of our age (Isaiah 6:8), we have isolated ourselves behind the walls of a vast evangelical ghetto. We have rendered unto Caesar everything—what is Caesar's *and* what is God's.

Meanwhile, the modern day party of the Herodians is busy with its work of oppression and repression. The Herodians hold seats of power: in government, in education, in the media, in the judiciary, and in the financial world. They care nothing for the evangelicals' morality. They abhor our puritanical virtues. They chafe against our piety. They despise our nonconformity.

But, they applaud our *irrelevancy*. They appreciate our distraction from the things of this world. They know that as long as we separate God and state, *they* will continue to have a free reign. They will be able to perpetuate their slaughter of the unborn, their assault on the family, and their defamation of all things holy, all things sacred, and all things pure. They will be able to transfer deity and rule from God to themselves, "doing what is right in their own eyes" (Judges 20:25). In this way, these Herodians (or secular humanists, as we call them today) count the irrelevant, isolationist evangelical Church as their most trusted ally.

They couldn't do what they do without us.

Conclusion

The second basic principle in the Biblical blueprint for political action is that God has *ordained* civil government, thus making it a sacred institution. It is *God's* institution. Since it is our duty to "render unto God the things that are God's" (Matthew 22:21; Mark 12:17; Luke 20:25), we must work diligently to render unto Him "the powers that be" (Romans 13:1).

The Pharisees and Herodians both opposed Jesus on this matter. They both argued for a wall of separation between God and the state. The Pharisees avoided politics for fear it would pollute true religion. The Herodians avoided true religion for fear it would pollute politics. Together they saw in Jesus a real danger: the authoritative rule of God in *all* matters.

It should not surprise us then that the heirs of the Pharisees and Herodians should oppose Christ's disciples today as they follow in the footsteps of Joseph, Gideon, Deborah, Samuel, David, Nehemiah, and Daniel. It should not surprise us that they are alarmed when we affirm that political action is no less a divine arena for the proving of righteousness than is the family or the Church.

Politics is dirty. But only because we have left it to the Pharisees and Herodians for so long.

Summary

Jesus said to "Render unto Caesar the things that are Caesar's and unto God the things that are God's" (Luke 20:25), thus affirming both the legitimacy of the state and the limitation of the state.

Because God ordains civil government, the magistrates *have* real authority. But at the same time, they are *under* authority.

But more importantly, because God ordains civil government, it is a sacred institution and an honorable and holy vocational field. Christians should then view political action as a ministry as valid as any family ministry or church ministry.

A large number of the heroes of the Bible exercised their service to God in the political sphere.

Those who oppose godly political involvement, like the Pharisees and the Herodians, do so on the basis of an imagined wall of separation between God and the state.

That separation simply doesn't exist.

Our *hesitation* to take up the banner of the Living God shouldn't, either.

3

SINS OF COMMISSION

> I marvel that you are turning away so soon from Him who called you in the grace of Christ, to a different gospel, which is not another; but there are some who trouble you and want to pervert the gospel of Christ. But even if we, or an angel from heaven, preach any other gospel to you than what we have preached to you, let him be accursed. As we have said before, so now I say again, if anyone preaches any other gospel to you than what you have received, let him be accursed (Galatians 1:6-9).

Somehow the Christians in the Galatian church had been "bewitched" (Galatians 3:1). They had fallen into the grips of that most ancient of all heresies: *salvation by law.*

Galatia was a huge Roman province in the central mountainous region of Asia Minor. On his first missionary journey, the Apostle Paul had founded a number of churches there: in Antioch (Acts 13:14-52), in Iconium (Acts 14:1-7), in Lystra (Acts 14:8-18), and in Derbe (Acts 14:19-20). Later he would make at least two follow up visits (Acts 16:6; 18:23) so that the entire region was evangelized (Acts 19:10) and "the Word of the Lord grew mightily and was prevailing" (Acts 19:20).

Shortly after Paul's departure, however, a number of Jewish teachers arrived in Galatia. Whereas Paul had taught salvation "by grace through faith" and this alone, these men insisted that non-Jewish converts must also be circumcised and observe the Law in order to be saved. They contradicted Paul and the message of the Gospel, saying that faith is not enough, that there are things we must do to *merit* God's grace.

25

119:160) and that "the Word of our God shall stand forever" (Isaiah 40:8).

Jesus was affirming that unlike human lawmakers, God does not change His mind or alter His standards: "My covenant I will not violate, nor will I alter the utterance of my lips" (Psalm 89:34). When the Lord speaks, His Word stands firm forever. His assessments of right and wrong do not change from age to age: "All His precepts are trustworthy. They are established forever and ever, to be performed with faithfulness and uprightness" (Psalm 111:7-8).

Jesus appealed to the Law to bolster His teaching (John 8:17). He used it to vindicate His behavior (Matthew 12:5). He used it to answer His questioners (Luke 10:26), to indict His opponents (John 7:19), to identify God's will (Matthew 19:17), to establish Kingdom citizenship (Matthew 7:24), to confront Satan (Matthew 4:1-11), and to confirm Christian love (John 14:21). He was, in short, a *champion of the Law.*

But He also put the Law in its place. He showed us that Law is not designed to effect *salvation* for men. Instead, it is designed to effect *dominion* for men. It is designed to enable men to submit to and evidence the rule of God.

This is what the Apostle Paul meant when he said that we are no longer "under the law" (Romans 6:14-15), that in fact we are "dead to the law" (Romans 7:4; Galatians 2:19). Instead, we are *under* the sacrificial covering of Christ's blood, fulfilling the death sentence of the law against us (Romans 8:1-2). But Law is not made void; rather, its curse is (Galatians 3:13). In fact, when the Law is put in its proper place, it is "established" (Romans 3:31).

The Law is established by grace to accomplish several tasks in the theocracy of heaven and earth:

First, the Law reveals the moral standards of God's rule. This is what the early Church fathers and the reformers called *usus politicus*: the civil application of Law.

> How can a young man keep his way pure? By keeping it according to Thy Word. With all my heart I have sought Thee; do not let me wander from Thy commandments. Thy Word I have

treasured in my heart, that I may not sin against Thee. Blessed art Thou, O Lord; teach me Thy statutes (Psalm 119:9-12).

And all these blessings shall come upon you and overtake you, if you will obey the Lord your God. Blessed shall you be in the city, and blessed shall you be in the country. Blessed shall be the offspring of your body and the produce of your ground and the offspring of your beasts, the increase of your herd and the young of your flock. Blessed shall be your basket and your kneading bowl. Blessed shall you be when you come in, and blessed shall you be when you go out. The Lord will cause your enemies who rise up against you to be defeated before you; they shall come out against you one way and shall flee before you seven ways.

But it shall come about, if you will not obey the Lord your God, to observe to do all His commandments and His statutes with which I charge you today, that all these curses shall come upon you and overtake you. Cursed shall you be in the city, and cursed shall you be in the country. Cursed shall be your basket and your kneading bowl, cursed shall be the offspring of your body and the produce of your ground, the increase of your herd and the young of your flock. Cursed shall you be when you come in, and cursed shall you be when you go out (Deuteronomy 28:2-7, 15-19).

Second, the Law convicts us of sin and leads us to Christ. This is what the early Church fathers and the reformers called *usus pedagogus*: the tutorial application of Law.

Therefore the Law has become our tutor to lead us to Christ, that we may be justified by faith (Galatians 3:24).

What shall we say then? Is the Law sin? May it never be! On the contrary, I would not have come to know sin except through the Law; for I would not have known about coveting if the Law had not said, "You shall not covet." But sin, taking opportunity through the commandment, produced in me coveting of every kind; for apart from the Law sin is dead. And I was once alive apart from the Law; but when the commandment came, sin became alive, and I died; and this commandment, which was to result in life, proved to result in death for me; for sin, taking opportunity through the commandment, deceived me, and through it killed me. So then, the Law is holy, and the commandment is holy and righteous and good.

Therefore did that which is good become a cause of death for
me? May it never be! Rather it was sin, in order that it might be
shown to be sin by effecting my death through that which is good,
that through the commandment sin might become utterly sinful.
For we know that the Law is spiritual; but I am of flesh, sold into
bondage to sin. For that which I am doing, I do not understand;
for I am not practicing what I would like to do, but I am doing the
very thing I hate. But if I do the very thing I do not wish to do, I
agree with the Law, confessing that it is good (Romans 7:7-16).

Third, the Law is a testimony to the nations, calling them to
repentance. This is what the early Church fathers and the reformers called *usus motivatus*: the motivational application of Law.

See, I have taught you statutes and judgments just as the Lord
my God commanded me, that you should do thus in the land
where you are entering to possess it. So keep and do them, for that
is your wisdom and your understanding in the sight of the peoples
who will hear all these statutes and say, "Surely this great nation is
a wise and understanding people." For what great nation is there
that has a god so near to it as is the Lord our God whenever we call
on Him? Or what great nation is there that has statutes and judgments as righteous as this whole law which I am setting before you
today (Deuteronomy 4:5-8)?

I am the Lord. I have called you in righteousness, I will also
hold you by the hand and watch over you, and I will appoint you
as a covenant to the people, as a light to the nations, to open blind
eyes, to bring out prisoners from the dungeons, and those who
dwell in darkness from the prison (Isaiah 42:6-7).

And the Lord has today declared you to be His people, a treasured possession, as He promised you, and that you should keep
all His commandments; and that He shall set you high above all
nations which He has made, for praise, fame, and honor; and that
you shall be a consecrated people to the Lord your God, as He has
spoken (Deuteronomy 26:18-19).

Fourth, the Law is a blueprint for living, a means for attaining
our promised victory. This is what the early Church fathers and
the reformers called *usus normativus*: the practical and normative
application of Law.

All Scripture is inspired by God and profitable for teaching, for reproof, for correction, for training in righteousness; that the man of God may be adequate, equipped for every good work (2 Timothy 3:16-17).

His divine power has granted to us everything pertaining to life and godliness, through the true knowledge of Him who called us by His own glory and excellence. For by these He has granted to us His precious and magnificent promises, in order that by them you might become partakers of the divine nature, having escaped the corruption that is in the world by lust (2 Peter 1:3-4).

Only be strong and very courageous; be careful to do according to all the law which Moses My servant commanded you; do not turn from it to the right or to the left, so that you may have success wherever you go. This book of the Law shall not depart from your mouth, but you shall meditate on it day and night, so that you may be careful to do according to all that is written in it; for then you will make your way prosperous, and then you will have success (Joshua 1:7-8).

So, far from being a replacement for grace, or being opposed to grace, the Bible teaches that the Law is a *provision of grace.* "Is the Law contrary to the promises of God? God forbid" (Galatians 3:21).

Sadly, the Galatians objected to this balanced Biblical perspective of the Law.

Manipulating God

The primary difference between Biblical faith and heresy is that true religion is *a response to truth* and false religion is *an attempt to manipulate God.* True faith aims at God's satisfaction, while heresy aims at self satisfaction.

Throughout the ages, men like Cain have *used* religion to get what they want (Genesis 4:3-8; Hebrews 11:4; 1 John 3:12). Men like Balaam have *used* religion to control circumstances (Numbers 31:16; 2 Peter 2:15; Revelation 2:14). Men like Korah have *used* religion to enhance their position (Numbers 16:1-3; 31-35). Cain, Balaam, and Korah all believed in the *universal power* of Law. They believed that not only could they manipulate human society

and natural elements with Law, but that God would also be forced
to conform Himself to the desires and demands of men who act in
terms of Law: If men will say certain things, do certain things, believe certain things, or act out certain things, then God will *have to*
respond. In essence, they believed that *man* controlled his own
destiny, using *rituals* and *formulas* of Law like *magic* to save mankind, to shape history, to govern society, and to manipulate God.

It seems that men are forever rejecting the grace of God,
"going the way of Cain, rushing headlong into the error of
Balaam, and perishing in the rebellion of Korah" (Jude 11). That
is the reason why statism is so predominant among rebellious men
and nations. For if Law *can* save mankind, shape history, govern
society, and manipulate God, then obviously men must work to
institute a total Law-Order. If the rituals and formulas of Law are
indeed like magic, then men must erect a comprehensive state to
govern men comprehensively. Communism is a saving Law-
Order. It attempts to rule *every* aspect of life and to solve every di-
lemma of life through the agency of the omnipotent, omnipresent
state. Likewise, modern liberalism attempts to create a messianic
state, offering salvation by Law. It attempts to create a top-down
government, manufacturing salvation by legislation. Whenever
any problem arises, instead of relying upon Almighty God and
His guidance in the Word, advocates of the liberal state rush to
the bar with a whole series of new rules, regulations, and laws.

Christian Political Action

Christians must reject the conception of salvation by legislation as the heresy that it is. We must reject the notion of salvation
by Law as "another Gospel" (Galatians 1:6), a false Gospel.

Christian political action is a *response* to truth. It is a *response* to
the rule of God. It is *not* an attempt to control men and elements
by force. It is instead an attempt to reveal the grace of God
through *usus politicus, usus pedagogus, usus motivatus,* and *usus normativus.*

Christians do *not* believe that if we could only pass a few good
laws, or elect a few good legislators, or appoint a few good judges,

all would be well with the world. Christians do not believe in salvation by legislation or salvation by politics. To believe that would be to repeat the Galatian error. To believe that would be to mimic the sins of Cain, Balaam, and Korah. To believe that would be to invite statist tyranny.

Christian political action does not put its trust in legal, judicial, or mechanical messiahs. Its trust is in the one true Messiah, "the only mediator between God and man" (1 Timothy 2:5), Jesus Christ.

Thus, Christian political action is a recognition and submission to the rule of God. It is a rendering unto Him the things that are His, and above all it is a visible manifestation in the civil sphere of the *grace* of God.

Conclusion

The third basic principle in the Biblical blueprint for political action is that salvation by Law is the most ancient of all heresies. It is an Old Testament heresy *and* a New Testament heresy.

Man is saved "by grace through faith" (Ephesians 2:8). Any attempt to bypass that fundamental reliance on the mercy of God is the most rank form of rebellion.

The Law was intended by God to be a way of life for us, *not* a way of salvation. It was designed to be the effect of salvation, *not* the cause of it. That is why unlike the Communists or the modern liberals, Christians do not rely on an all-encompassing messianic state to solve all the problems of society. Christians do not believe in the power of legislation, but in the power of God.

Thus, Christians are politically active *because* of salvation, *not* in order to *provoke* salvation.

Summary

The Galatian church, bewitched by Jewish legalists, began to believe that in order to be saved, men must do *something more* than trust the mercy and grace of God. They began to believe in salvation by Law.

Salvation by Law is a heresy. All through the Bible from Genesis to Revelation, God makes it clear that "justification is by faith" (Habakkuk 2:4) and by faith *alone*.

The Law is still valid, though. It is valid as a blueprint for living: revealing God's standards, leading us to Christ, motivating the nations, directing our service.

Those who reject this balanced view use the Law to manipulate God and control events to their own advantage.

The inevitable result of legalism is statist tyranny.

On the other hand, the inevitable result of Christian political action is revival.

"If My people who are called by My name humble themselves and pray, and seek My face and turn from their wicked ways, then I will hear from heaven and forgive their sins, and will *heal their land*" (2 Chronicles 7:14).

Christians must be cognizant of this truth. And we must *act* accordingly.

4

SINS OF OMISSION

Then the men rose from there and looked toward Sodom, and Abraham went with them to send them on the way. And the Lord said, "Shall I hide from Abraham what I am doing, since Abraham shall surely become a great and mighty nation, and all the nations of the earth shall be blessed in him? For I have known him, in order that he may command his children and his household after him, that they keep the way of the Lord, to do righteousness and justice, that the Lord may bring to Abraham what He has spoken to him." And the Lord said, "Because the outcry against Sodom and Gomorrah is great, and because their sin is very grievous, I will go down now and see whether they have done altogether according to the outcry against it that has come to Me; and if not, I will know." Then the men turned away from there and went toward Sodom, but Abraham still stood before the Lord (Genesis 18:16-22).

The cities of Sodom and Gomorrah were consumed with vile and detestable sin. The people were perverse (Genesis 19:5). They were violent (Genesis 19:9). They were arrogant, careless, and selfish (Ezekiel 16:49). They were haughty, self-destructive, and abominable (Ezekiel 16:50). They were utterly wicked (Genesis 18:20).

But that is not why God destroyed them.

Despite all the debauchery, lasciviousness, and blasphemy, God was willing to spare the cities.

And Abraham came near and said, "Wilt Thou indeed sweep away the righteous with the wicked? Suppose there are fifty righteous within the city; wilt Thou indeed sweep it away and not spare the place for the sake of the fifty righteous who are in it? Far be it from Thee to do such a thing, to slay the righteous with the wicked, so that the righteous and the wicked are treated alike. Far be it from Thee! Shall not the Judge of all the earth deal justly?" So the Lord said, "If I find in Sodom fifty righteous within the city, then I will spare the whole place on their account" (Genesis 18:23-26).

If there were but fifty men guarding the city with their righteousness, God would relent.

And Abraham answered and said, "Now behold, I have ventured to speak to the Lord, although I am but dust and ashes. Suppose the fifty righteous are lacking five, wilt Thou destroy the whole city because of five?" And He said, "I will not destroy it if I find forty-five there" (Genesis 18:27-28).

Again, God told Abraham, He would spare the cities if only there were forty-five men guarding the people with their righteousness.

And he spoke to Him yet again and said, "Suppose forty are found there?" And He said, "I will not do it on account of the forty" (Genesis 18:29).

Once again, God would acknowledge the preserving power of forty righteous men.

Then he said, "Oh may the Lord not be angry, and I shall speak; suppose thirty are found there?" And He said, "I will not do it if I find thirty there" (Genesis 18:30).

Even "a little leaven leavens the whole lump" (1 Corinthians 5:6). God told Abraham that He would not judge the city on account of the protection afforded by thirty righteous men.

And he said, "Now behold, I have ventured to speak to the Lord; suppose twenty are found there?" And He said, "I will not destroy it on account of the twenty" (Genesis 18:31).

Even twenty guardians were enough to stay the hand of execution.

Then he said, "Oh may the Lord not be angry, and I shall speak only this once; suppose ten are found there?" And He said,

"I will not destroy it on account of the ten." And as soon as He had finished speaking to Abraham the Lord departed; and Abraham returned to his place (Genesis 18:32-33).

The moral of this seemingly tedious lesson is abundantly clear: if the righteous will *guard* the cities, they are safe. But, if there are no guardians, disaster is inevitable.

Priesthood and Guardianship

God calls His people to be priests. The Israelites were to be "a nation of priests" (Exodus 19:6). And since the Church has inherited the promises, privileges, and place of Israel (Romans 2:28-29), God has called us to be a "nation of priests" as well (1 Peter 2:5; Revelation 1:6; 5:10).

The word "priest" literally means "guardian." Thus a priest is someone who *guards*. He protects. He preserves. He stays the hand of destruction and defilement.

Adam was called to be a priest. He was to "cultivate and *guard* the garden" (Genesis 2:15). But he failed to do his duty and the fall resulted (Genesis 3:1-20).

Aaron was called to be a priest. He was to *guard* the people from sin and shame (Exodus 32:25). But he failed to do his duty and the people began to worship and revel before a golden calf (Exodus 32:1-6).

The Levites were called to be priests. Why? Because they *guarded* the integrity of God when all the rest of Israel was consumed with idolatry (Exodus 32:26-29). It was not until the Levites failed to the uttermost that God brought condemnation and judgement upon Israel (Jeremiah 6:13-15).

Man was *made* to be a priest before God. He was *made* to guard against evil.

Thus, the *inclination* to priesthood is inescapable. Even if man fails, as Adam, Aaron, and the Levites ultimately did, the *impulse* to guard remains. If man fails to be a *true* priest guarding the *true* sanctuary, he will become a *false* priest, guarding a *false* sanctuary.

When Cain was cast out from the presence of the Lord (Genesis 4:12), he settled in the land of "wandering" (Genesis 4:16).

fathers to integrate devoted Christians into the political life. (See especially Charles Hyneman and Donald Lutz's two volume set: *American Political Writing During the Founding Era 1760-1805*, Liberty Press, 1983; and Verna M. Hall's superb multi-volume set: *The Christian History of the Constitution of the Unites States of America*, The Foundation for American Christian Education, 1960, 1962, 1966, 1969.) They understood that "where the Spirit of the Lord is, there is liberty" (2 Corinthians 3:17).

Now, to be sure, those early Americans did not desire to establish an *ecclesiocracy*, where the clergy controls the state. Ecclesiocracy has been denounced and rejected by Bible-believing Christians ever since the medieval era.

But then neither did they desire to establish a *democracy*, where the majority controls the state. Democracy too has been denounced and rejected by Bible-believing Christians ever since the medieval era.

They did not desire either the tyranny of the cloth nor the tyranny of the fifty-one percent.

Instead, they sought to imitate the Hebrew *theocratic republic*. They wanted a popular representative government that *guarded* and *preserved* "life, liberty and the pursuit of happiness" by means of priestly righteousness. Consequently, nearly all the distinctive ideas of the American Constitution were derived from the Scriptures: the balance of powers (Exodus 12:21, 28; Numbers 11:16-17, 24-26), the upper and lower legislatures (Numbers 10:2-4), the covenant of rights (Deuteronomy 28:1-68), the electoral college (Numbers 1:16; 16:2), the popular vote (Exodus 19:7-9), and the chief executive (Numbers 27:1-9).

The Christian men who so obviously searched the Scriptures for these principles struggled long and hard against the influences of Deism, Unitarianism, Free Masonry, and Transcendentalism. That they prevailed by and large is a testament to the power of salt. That they prevailed by and large is a testament to the critical importance of the priestly work. That they prevailed by and large is a testament to the value of Christian political action.

Had Sodom and Gomorrah had such men guarding them with

righteousness, they might still be here, flourishing, with liberty and justice for all.

And if we had such men in America today, we would not be in such dire straits morally, economically, and politically.

Conclusion

The fourth basic principle in the Biblical blueprint for political action is that we must guard the land. It is our priestly task.

Without our preserving and restraining activity, the land is doomed. Like Sodom and Gomorrah it will perish under the hand of God's judgement, all for the lack of a few righteous men.

God has called us to "stand in the gap" (Ezekiel 22:30), seasoning the earth as salt. To abandon that task is to commit a most disastrous sin — a sin of omission.

It is critical for the very *survival* of our children and our children's children that we follow in the footsteps of Joseph, Nehemiah, Mordecai, Daniel, and the American founding fathers, exercising priestly guardianship in the political arena.

Summary

Sodom and Gomorrah were not destroyed simply because they were evil. God judged those cities with fire and brimstone because not even ten righteous men could be found to guard them.

God made it clear to Abraham that when there are no guardians, judgment is inevitable.

God has appointed His people to be the priests, or guardians, of the earth.

Adam was to be a priest, as were Aaron and the Levites. But each of them failed to do his duty properly, and as a result, destruction came upon the land.

The call to the priesthood has not ever been stilled. Jesus has passed the mantle of Israel to His disciples.

Now *we* are to be the salt of the earth, preserving it from sin and serving it as faithful priests.

"bless those" who blessed him and "curse those" who cursed him
(Genesis 12:3) and to "bless" him all the days of his life (Genesis
12:2). But central to *all* these promises was the *one promise*: the
promise of *land*.

God chose Abram to "go forth" out of Ur of the Chaldees and
from his "relatives" and from his "father's house" in order to take
possession of *land* (Genesis 12:1).

> And the Lord appeared to Abram and said, "To your descen-
> dants I will give this land" (Genesis 12:7).

> For all the land which you see, I will give it to you and to your
> descendants forever. Arise, walk about the land through its length
> and breadth; for I will give it to you (Genesis 13:15, 17).

> And I will give to you and to your descendants after you, the
> land of your sojournings, all the land of Canaan, for an everlasting
> possession, and I will be their God (Genesis 17:8).

> By faith Abraham, when he was called, obeyed by going out to
> a land which he was to receive for an inheritance; and he went out,
> not knowing where he was going. By faith he lived as an alien in
> the land of promise, as in a foreign land, dwelling in tents with
> Isaac and Jacob, fellow heirs of the same promise; for he was look-
> ing for the city which has foundations, whose architect and builder
> is God (Hebrews 11:8-10).

Land was central to the promise God gave Abram, and it was
central to the mission God gave him, as well. The promised land
was promised *land*. (See Gary North's book in the Biblical Blueprints Series, *Inherit the Earth: Biblical Principles for Economics*.)

The Land

Land and faith in the Bible are interrelated in three essential
ways.

First, land gives us a place to worship. It affords us with a holy
place where we can draw into God's presence and render him due
honor and praise. It provides us with a *sanctuary*.

In the beginning "God planted a garden" (Genesis 2:8). It was
lush with "every tree that is pleasing to the sight and good for

food" (Genesis 2:9), and it was lavishly irrigated by the headwaters of four great rivers (Genesis 2:10). "In the midst" of this luxuriant garden God placed "the tree of life" and "the tree of the knowledge of good and evil," thus establishing His sacramental presence (Genesis 2:9). God set aside this *land* so that He could meet with man, ordaining true worship, true fellowship, and true *sanctuary.*

Second, land gives us a place to rest. It affords us with a dwelling place where we can retire into the comfortable confines of the family hearth. It provides us with a *home.*

The garden sanctuary was located in the easternmost corner of the land of Eden (Genesis 2:8). That land was a vast mountainous domain (Ezekiel 28:14) that, like the garden, was well watered, lavishly stocked, gloriously adorned, and fabulously furnished (Genesis 2:10-14). It was a genuine paradise laden high with precious stones, jewels, and minerals (Ezekiel 28:13). God placed man in the midst of this paradise to live out his days establishing a godly seed. God set aside this *land* so that man could have a *home.*

Third, land gives us a place to work. It affords us with an arena for the practical outworking of our faith. It provides us with *dominion.*

The garden was set in the midst of Eden (Genesis 2:8), and Eden was set in the midst of the world (Genesis 2:10-14). It was there in the various outlying lands of the world that man was to exercise authority and diligence bringing to bear God's order and purpose for all things (Genesis 1:26). The lands of Havilah (Genesis 2:11), Cush (Genesis 2:13), and Assyria (Genesis 2:14) were rich and good, but they needed the subordinated rule of God in man (Genesis 1:28). So, God set aside *land* so that man could work and take *dominion* over the earth.

The Pattern of Digression

When man sinned against God, not only did *he* fall (Genesis 3:7), but the *land* fell as well (Genesis 3:17-19). Not only were *the sons of men* shackled to "bodies of sin and death" (Romans 7:24), but the *land* was "subjected to futility" (Romans 8:20) and "enslaved to corruption" as well (Romans 8:21). Man lost his inheritance, his *land*.

First, man lost his *sanctuary-land*. As a consequence of his sin, man was expelled from the garden (Genesis 3:23). Access to the presence of God was cut off (Genesis 3:24). Man could only worship God "from afar" (Exodus 24:1-2).

Next, man lost his *home-land*. Sin continued to progress in the sons of men. When Cain rose up and murdered his brother Abel (Genesis 4:8), he was driven out of his home in the same way that Adam and Eve were driven out of the sanctuary (Genesis 3:24-4:12). And whereas the land only yielded up its strength to Adam and Eve after great travail and difficulty (Genesis 3:17-19), it would not yield up its strength *at all* to Cain (Genesis 4:12). Thus, his sin sent him out homeless, as "a vagrant and wanderer on the earth" (Genesis 4:14).

Finally, man lost the *whole world*. The progression of sin's vile destruction continued even after Cain. Anarchy and wholesale murder became commonplace (Genesis 4:23-24). Debauchery and lust prevailed (Genesis 6:2-4). "The wickedness of man was great on the earth" (Genesis 6:5), so that even the wilderness of man's wanderings was laid waste. After much forbearance, God judged the land with a sweeping flood and the whole earth was lost (Genesis 7:17-24).

Whenever we rebel against God we set into motion this same sequence of events—this pattern of digression. First, we lose our *sanctuary*. Then we lose our *home*. And finally, if sin is left unchecked, we lose the whole *world*.

When Israel sinned by taking idols into its midst, God sent the overlords of Assyria to pillage and plunder the temple (2 Chronicles 28:20-21). They lost *the sanctuary*.

When the nation continued on, unrepentant, God sent the warlords of Babylon to sack and sunder the cities (2 Kings 5:1-4). And thus the people were exiled from their inheritance. They lost their *home*.

Finally, when the people remained stiff-necked in the face of even this, God scattered them to the four winds (2 Chronicles 36:11-21; 2 Kings 25:24-26). And thus they lost their *dominion*. They lost the whole world.

The same process was repeated again in the day of Christ. The Jews refused to submit to the Lord Jesus, preferring instead their Roman captivity (Matthew 23:1-39). So in A.D. 70 they lost their sanctuary (Matthew 24:1-2). They lost their home (Matthew 24:15-19). They lost everything (Matthew 24:20-28).

Again and again throughout the ages, the pattern of digression is repeated. The pages of history are littered with the tattered reminders that sin has very clear consequences (Galatians 6:7). Cultures that refuse to acknowledge God's rule suffer a downward spiral of judg.ment and loss. First they lose the privilege of worship. Then they lose their home. And finally, when sin has become fully mature, they lose the whole world.

What is absolutely frightening is that we can see the initial stages of this pattern of digression manifesting itself in America today. What with increasing state pressure and persecution on churches (sanctuary), and state interference and encroachment on families (home), the necessity of arresting our national sin and reaffirming the rule of God becomes all the more urgent.

The Pattern of Redemption

Because land and faith are so closely interrelated, it should not surprise us to discover that the history of God's redemptive work involves the reclamation of the earth *as well as* the restoration of mankind. "For God so loved the *world* that He gave His only begotten Son" (John 3:16).

Whenever God begins to restore His people He also sets us to the task of reclaiming the world, the home, and ultimately the sanctuary:

> For the anxious longing of the creation waits eagerly for the revealing of the sons of God. For the creation was subjected to futility, not of its own will, but because of Him who subjected it, in hope that the creation itself also will be set free from its slavery to corruption into the freedom of the glory of the children of God.

For we know that the whole creation groans and suffers the pains
of childbirth together until now (Romans 8:19-22).

This is why when God called Abram out of Ur of the Chaldees,
the task of reclaiming the land began immediately. Abram was
"saved by grace through faith" (Romans 4:3, Ephesians 2:8). But
he was saved for a purpose (Ephesians 2:10). And that purpose included undoing the curse of sin that had corrupted the earth
through an obedient application of God's rule in all things.

So, Abram began to exercise redemptive grace among the nations, in the *world* (Genesis 22:18). He became a blessing to the
people of Siddim (Genesis 14:1-24), the people of Gerar (Genesis
20:1-18), the people of Egypt (Genesis 21:1-21), the people of
Philistia (Genesis 21:22-34), the people of Canaan (Genesis
23:1-20), and the people of Mesopotamia (Genesis 24:1-67). He
began to *take dominion over the land*: digging wells (Genesis 21:25),
accumulating wealth (Genesis 13:2), conquering evil doers (Genesis 14:1-20), establishing alliances (Genesis 21:27-33), and staking
out the inheritance (Genesis 12:4-9). He began to *reclaim the world*.

Abram also began to restore the *home* of the people of God:

> By faith Abraham, when he was called, obeyed by going out to
> a place which he was to receive for an inheritance; and he went
> out, not knowing where he was going. By faith he lived as an alien
> in the land of promise, as in a foreign land, dwelling in tents with
> Isaac and Jacob, fellow heirs of the same promise; for he was look-
> ing for the city which has foundations, whose architect and builder
> is God (Hebrews 11:8-10).

He was looking for the city of rest (Hebrews 4:1-13), the city of
refuge, the *home* of God's chosen children. He trekked throughout
the land of promise marking out the territory city by city and site
by site (Genesis 12:4-9). In essence he was symbolically *conquering*
the land, for when Joshua led the army of Israel across the Jordan
later on, he followed the path that Abram had marked out 400
years before. Thus, Abram truly began to *reclaim the home*.

Finally, Abram began to restore true worship in the land. He
established sanctuaries everywhere he went, building altars and

memorials to the Lord (Genesis 12:4-9). He met with God at Shechem (Genesis 12:6), at Bethel (Genesis 12:8), at Hebron (Genesis 13:18), and at Moriah (Genesis 22:2), where the Jerusalem temple would later be built (2 Chronicles 3:1). Abram consecrated each of these sites to the Lord, establishing them as places of worship. He was thus, reclaiming the *sanctuary*.

Like the pattern of digression, this pattern of redemption recurs throughout the Bible and throughout history. When Israel returned to the land from the exodus they first reclaimed their dominion, then their home, and finally their sanctuary.

When Ezra and Nehemiah brought the people back from the Babylonian captivity, the pattern went into effect again. Dominion was reclaimed (Nehemiah 2:1-8), their home was reclaimed (Nehemiah 6:15-16), and finally the sanctuary was reclaimed (Haggai 1:12-15).

Whenever and wherever people respond to the grace of God, we are simultaneously lifted up from our fallen estate *and* commissioned to go forth and reclaim the land (Matthew 28:19-20; Romans 8:19-22). With great, great privilege comes great, great responsibility. We are to counter the pattern of digression with the pattern of redemption.

(For these insights into the life of Abraham, I am indebted to James B. Jordan's fine study, *The Life of Abraham*, available from Geneva Ministries, Box 131300, Tyler, Texas, 75713.)

The Task of Political Action

"The earth is the LORD's" (Psalm 24:1). That is clear enough. He executes *dominion* over it with "an everlasting dominion" (Daniel 4:3), and He *rules* it from His "throne on high" (Psalm 11:4). But at the same time, He graciously apportions it out to His people. He commissions *us* to exercise stewardship over it. He gives us *land*. And we are able to express His dominion by ordering and subduing that land. He gives us an *inheritance*. And we are to affirm His rule by forging out of that inheritance a harmonious *world*, a secure *home*, and a holy *sanctuary*.

This is the crux of Christian political action. This is the task

of Ur, it was to go forth and claim an inheritance of land. When
he established sanctuaries, forged alliances, dug wells, and conquered evil doers, he was attesting to the rule of God. He was
countering the effects of sin out in the *world*, in his *home*, and before *the altar* of God.

He was reclaiming the land.

This principle runs all through the Bible. God's redemptive
work involves more than saving souls. It involves more than preserving the status quo. It involves making *"all* things new"
(2 Corinthians 5:17). It involves taking "authority over the nations" with the applied rule of God (Revelation 2:27-28). It involves Christian political action.

Anything more or anything less simply cannot be warranted
from Scripture.

Summary

Abram was called by God to lay claim to a great inheritance.
That inheritance was a promise of dominion over all the nations
of the earth. It was a promise of a *land* and a future. Land and
faith in the Bible are interrelated in three essential ways:

First, land provides us with a *sanctuary*.

Second, land provides us with a *home*.

Third, land provides us with dominion out in the *world*.

When we rebel against God, we lose access to these privileges:
first, we lost the right to worship. Then we lose our home. And
finally we lose the whole world.

This pattern of digression runs throughout the Bible and
throughout history.

But there is another pattern in Scripture and history. It is the
pattern of redemption.

The task of the people of God is to counter the effects of sin
with the redemptive work of Christ. The task of the people of God
is to reclaim the land.

This is the crux of Christian political action.

We've become so heavenly minded that we're no earthly good.
The Gospel calls us to be so heavenly minded (Hebrews 3:1) that
we make the earth good (2 Corinthians 10:5).

6

THE STANDARD OF EXCELLENCE

> Select from all the people able men, such as fear God, men of truth, hating covetousness; and place such over them to be rulers of thousands, rulers of hundreds, rulers of fifties, and rulers of tens. And let them judge the people at all times. Then it will be that every great matter they shall bring to you, but every small matter they themselves shall judge. So it will be easier for you, for they will bear the burden with you (Exodus 18:21-22).

Moses was facing a political crisis. The governmental apparatus of the nation had begun to bog down. Justice was impaired. Administration was slowed. And services were stymied.

Jethro, Moses' father-in-law, suggested that the entire civil structure be reformed to accord with God's will (Exodus 18:23). He said that all the people, being the priests of God, commissioned as they were to be salt and light, should be taught the statues and the laws of God (Exodus 18:20). And then, according to Jethro, they should exercise their responsibilities as righteous citizens (Exodus 18:18). Men should be selected out of the midst of the holy congregation he said, who could exercise the *ministry of political action* (Exodus 18:21).

But these men had to adhere to certain standards before they could be considered for this ministry. Their character had to be tested. They had to be screened by the Law. To *govern* in terms of the covenant, first they had to *be governed* in terms of the covenant. To *judge*, first they had to be judged. Those who are not willing to be judged by God's law are warned not to execute judgment: "Judge not, that you be not judged. For with what judgment you judge, you will be judged; and with the same measure you use, it will be measured back to you" (Matthew 7:1-2).

So, what were the terms of judgment? What were the Biblical prerequisites for exercising the ministry of political action? What political standard did the men have to adhere to?

God-Fearers

First, they had to adhere to the *Biblical standard of godliness*. They had to be men who feared God (Exodus 18:21). According to Jethro, this is an inescapable prerequisite. After all:

> The fear of the Lord is the beginning of wisdom; a good understanding have all those who do His commandments. His praise endures forever (Psalm 111:10).

> The fear of the Lord is the beginning of knowledge, but fools despise wisdom and instruction (Proverbs 1:7).

> The fear of the Lord prolongs days, but the years of the wicked will be shortened (Proverbs 10:27).

> In the fear of the Lord there is strong confidence, and His children will have a place of refuge. The fear of the Lord is a fountain of life, to avoid the snares of death (Proverbs 14:26-27).

> Better is a little with the fear of the Lord, than great treasure with trouble (Proverbs 15:16).

A nation whose leaders fear God will suffer no want (Psalm 34:9). It will ever be blest (Psalm 115:13). It will be set high above all the nations of the earth (Deuteronomy 28:1). Ancient Israel's greatness can be directly attributed to her leaders' fear of God: Abraham was a God-fearer (Genesis 20:11); Joseph was a God-fearer (Deuteronomy 10:12); as were Job (Job 41:23); Joshua (Joshua 24:14); David (2 Samuel 23:3); Jehoshaphat (2 Chronicles 19:4); Hezekiah (Jeremiah 26:19); Nehemiah (Nehemiah 5:15); and Jonah (Jonah 1:9).

Clearly, those who exercised the ministry of political action in Israel would likewise have to be God-fearers.

Men of Truth

Second, they had to adhere to the *Biblical standard of truthfulness*. They had to be men of honesty and integrity (Exodus 18:21). According to Jethro, this too is an inescapable prerequisite. After all:

> He who speaks truth declares righteousness, but a false witness, deceit. There is one who speaks like the piercings of a sword, but the tongue of the wise promotes health. The truthful lip shall be established forever, but a lying tongue is but for a moment. Deceit is in the heart of those who devise evil, but counselors of peace have joy. No grave trouble will overtake the righteous, but the wicked shall be filled with evil. Lying lips are an abomination to the Lord, but those who deal truthfully are His delight (Proverbs 12:17-22).

> Even though divination is on the lips of the king, his mouth must not transgress in judgement. It is an abomination for kings to commit wickedness, for a throne is established by righteousness. Righteous lips are the delight of kings, and they love him who speaks what is right (Proverbs 16:10, 12-13).

> Surely His salvation is near to those who fear Him, that glory may dwell in our land. Mercy and truth have met together; righteousness and peace have kissed each other. Truth shall spring out of the earth, and righteousness shall look down from heaven (Psalm 85:9-11).

God's people are commanded to worship Him in truth (John 4:24), serve Him in truth (Joshua 24:14), and walk before Him in truth (1 Kings 2:4). The nation that desires the blessing of God must have leaders who esteem the truth (Proverbs 23:3), love the truth (Zechariah 8:19), rejoice in the truth (1 Corinthians 13:6), meditate upon the truth (Philippians 4:8), and execute judgment with truth (Zechariah 8:16). For they who speak the truth show forth righteousness (Proverbs 12:17) and are the delight of God (Proverbs 12:22).

Truth sanctifies (John 17:17-19) and purifies (1 Peter 1:22) and thus ought to be acknowledged (2 Timothy 2:25), believed

(2 Thessalonians 2:12-13), obeyed (Romans 2:8), loved (2 Thessalonians 2:10), and manifested (2 Corinthians 4:2).

Clearly, those who exercised the ministry of political action in Israel would not only have to fear God, they would have to be scrupulously honest as well.

Selfless Servants

Third, they had to adhere to the *Biblical standard of selflessness*. They had to be men of impeccability, hating covetousness and dishonest gain (Exodus 18:21). According to Jethro, this too is an inescapable prerequisite. After all:

> Yes, they are greedy gods which never have enough. And they are shepherds who cannot understand; they all look to their own way, every one for his own gain, from his own territory (Isaiah 56:11).

> I, the Lord, search the heart, I test the mind, even to give every man according to his ways, and according to the fruit of his doings. As a partridge that broods but does not hatch, so is he who gets riches, but not by right; it will leave him in the midst of his days, and at his end he will be a fool (Jeremiah 17:10-11).

> Behold the proud, his soul is not upright in him; but the just shall live by his faith. Indeed, because he transgresses by wine, he is a proud man, and he does not stay at home. Because he enlarges his desire as hell, and he is like death, and cannot be satisfied, he gathers to himself all nations and heaps up for himself all peoples. Shall not all these take up a proverb against him, and a taunting riddle against him, and say, "Woe to him who increases what is not his—how long? And to him who loads himself with many pledges?" (Habakkuk 2:4-6).

> For what is a man profited if he gains the whole world, and loses his own soul? Or what will a man give in exchange for his soul? (Matthew 16:26).

Covetous leaders often brought calamity upon the entire nation of Israel: Balaam, in loving the wages of unrighteousness (2 Peter 2:15); Achan, in hiding the contraband treasure of Jericho (Joshua 7:21); Eli's sons, in taking the flesh of the sacrifice (1 Samuel 8:3); Saul, in sparing Agag and the booty of war (1 Samuel

15:8-9); Ahab, in desiring Naboth's vineyard (1 Kings 21:2-16); and Judas, in swiping from the purse (John 12:6).

Selfless leaders, on the other hand, often brought great blessing upon the nation: Abraham, in according to Lot first choice in the land of Canaan (Genesis 13:9); Moses, in choosing to suffer affliction with his people rather than enjoy the passing pleasures of sin (Hebrews 11:25); Samuel, in his administration of justice (1 Samuel 12:3-4); the widow of Zarephath, in sharing with Elijah the last of her sustenance (1 Kings 17:12-15); Daniel, in refusing rewards from Belshazzar (Daniel 5:16-17); and Esther in risking her life for the deliverance of her people (Esther 4:16).

Clearly, those who exercised the ministry of political action in Israel would not only have to fear God and maintain strict honesty, they would have to serve in utter selflessness as well.

Able Men

But taking priority over these three essential character traits, Jethro made it clear to Moses that the men who were selected out of the congregation to serve in civil government had to be men of ability (Exodus 18:21). They had to adhere to the *Biblical standard of excellence*. They had to demonstrate wisdom, discernment, understanding, and sheer skill.

God granted Joseph great success as a leader because he combined godliness, truthfulness, and selflessness with evident *excellence* (Genesis 39:6). Everything he did prospered in his hand (Genesis 39:3). He served with excellence in Potiphar's household (Genesis 39:5). He served with excellence in the Egyptian prison (Genesis 39:22). He served with excellence in Pharaoh's court (Genesis 41:37-45). Joseph was not a dullard who was able to *get by* in this world simply because he had the love of God in his heart. He *changed* the world because he worked *out* what God had worked *in* (Philippians 2:12-13).

Similarly, God granted Nehemiah great success as a leader because he combined godliness, truthfulness, and selflessness with evident *excellence* (Nehemiah 2:18). Everything he did prospered in his hand (Nehemiah 13:14, 22, 31). He served with ex-

be afraid; For YAH, the Lord, is my strength and my song; He also has become my salvation." And in that day you will say: "Praise the Lord, call upon His name; declare His deeds among the peoples, make mention that His name is exalted. Sing to the Lord, for He has done excellent things; this is known in all the earth" (Isaiah 12:1-2, 4-5).

Your right hand, O Lord, has become glorious in power; Your right hand, O Lord, has dashed the enemy in pieces. And in the greatness of Your excellence You have overthrown those who rose against You; You sent forth Your wrath which consumed them like stubble. Fear and dread will fall on them; by the greatness of your arm they will be as still as a stone, till Your people pass over, O Lord, till the people pass over whom You have purchased (Exodus 15:6-7, 16).

His *will* is perfect:

God is clothed in fearful splendor: He, Shaddai, is far beyond our reach. Supreme in power, in equity, excelling in justice and in willful purpose toward men (Job 37:22-23).

And do not be conformed to this world, but be transformed by the renewing of your mind, that you may prove what is that good and acceptable and perfect will of God (Romans 12:2).

His *great and mighty deeds* are excellent:

Sing to the Lord, for He has done excellent things; this is known in all the earth. Cry out and shout, O inhabitant of Zion, for great is the Holy One of Israel in your midst! (Isaiah 12:5-6).

Great and marvelous are Your works, Lord God Almighty! Just and true are Your ways, O King of the saints! Who shall not fear You, O Lord, and glorify Your name? For You alone are holy. For all nations shall come and worship before You, for Your judgments have been manifested (Revelation 15:3-4).

His *ways* are excellent:

He has made His counsel excellent and His wisdom great (Isaiah 28:29, NASV).

As for God, His way is perfect; the Word of the Lord is proven; He is a shield to all who trust in Him. For who is God, except the Lord? And who is a rock, except our God?" (2 Samuel 22:31-32).

From cover to cover the Bible is a pantheon of praise to the *excellencies* of our God.

Called to Excellence

As God's representatives before men (2 Corinthians 5:20), we are to "proclaim His excellencies" (1 Peter 2:9). But our proclamation must not merely be "in word or with tongue, but in deed and with truth" (1 John 3:18). We proclaim *His* excellence by *our* excellence. In everything we do and in everything we say, we are to *manifest* Him who has "called us by His own glory and excellence" (2 Peter 1:3). As we follow after Him (Matthew 4:19), as we walk in His footsteps (1 Peter 2:21), and as we imitate His attributes (1 Peter 1:16), *excellence* is to be our hallmark. Like Jethro, Joseph, Nehemiah, Daniel, and even God Himself, we are to be noted for our excellencies.

God *expects* nothing less of us.

He who long ago demanded excellent sacrifices (Malachi 1:8-10), excellent artistry (Exodus 28:2), and excellent service (Proverbs 12:4), has in no way altered His standards of discipleship. We are to live lives marked by moral excellence (2 Peter 1:5). We are to keep our behavior excellent at all times (1 Peter 1:12). Our minds are to dwell constantly on excellence (Philippians 4:8). We are to walk in the way of excellence (1 Corinthians 12:31), manifesting cultural excellence (Genesis 1:28), economic excellence (Matthew 25:14-30), familial excellence (Proverbs 31:10-31), spiritual excellence (Philippians 1:10), and evangelistic excellence (Matthew 28:18-20). Mediocrity and triviality are to be the farthest things from the experience of faithful Christians.

The great God of *excellence* calls us to be men and women of *excellence* (1 Thessalonians 4:1, 10). Just as God called those under Moses and Jethro to excellence, He calls us to be men and women of *ability* (Exodus 18:21).

Unfortunately, the modern evangelical Church has failed to heed this call. It has almost become an evangelical legacy to churn out the basest sort of triviality: sloppy literature, sloppy music, sloppy social outreach, sloppy scholarship, sloppy worship, and sloppy political action. It seems that we have become "addicted to mediocrity." The liberal humanists can scoff at our legislative initiatives, slander our hand-picked candidates, scorn our most precious causes, subvert our judicial agendas, and scandalize our most important issues because we have failed to *excel*. We have failed to raise up and train up young Josephs, Nehemiahs, and Daniels. We have failed to take note of and emulate the excellencies of Almighty God. In short, we have failed to heed the high call of diligent discipleship.

That is why we must be clearheaded about our political agenda: Yes, God rules; yes, He has ordained politics as a legitimate sphere for ministry; yes, He has called us to be salt and light, redeeming the land as priests unto Him; but—if we pursue dominion in the same sloppy, shoddy way we've done everything else, we'd best forget about it altogether.

The fact is, if Christians gained control over the government of the United States tomorrow, our nation would be in *real trouble*. We simply do not yet have men and women of ability. We do not yet have men and women weaned on a legacy of excellence.

Not yet.

But, if we are to heed Christ's commands to render unto Him all things, to reclaim the land for Him, and to disciple the nations, teaching them to observe all that He has commanded (Matthew 28:20), then it is high time we returned to the standard of Jethro and Moses, the standard of Joseph, Nehemiah, and Daniel. It is high time we returned to the Biblical standard of excellence.

Conclusion

The sixth basic principle in the Biblical blueprint for political action is that we must return to the standard of excellence. God's earthly spokesmen must be governed by the Law of the covenant. Careless and haphazard moral tinkering by the "new right" will not be sufficient to return our nation to civil sanity. We must raise up leaders who know *what* to do and *how* to do it well.

The first major political crisis Moses faced after the exodus was a leadership vacuum. He simply could not do the job alone.

Therefore Jethro, his father-in-law, suggested that the entire civil structure of the fledgling Israelite nation be reformed. Why not appoint men from out of the midst of the congregation who could exercise the ministry of political action, he asked? Of course, he pointed out these appointees would have to be qualified: They would have to be godly men, trustworthy men, and men free of covetousness. And in addition to these prerequisites, they would have to be *able* men. The task of caring for the civil sphere is certainly too important to leave in the hands of the godless, the lecherous, and the greedy. But it is also too important to leave in the hands of the sloppy and careless.

It was on this foundation of excellence that Moses built the political action of the nation of Israel, and it is on that same foundation of excellence that we must build the political action of our own nation.

Summary

Jethro advised Moses to call men out of the congregation to exercise the ministry of political action, to lead the thousands, the hundreds, the fifties, and the tens.

It was necessary that these men be qualified.

First, they had to adhere to the Biblical standard of godliness. They had to be God-fearers.

Second, they had to adhere to the Biblical standard of truthfulness. They had to be men of honesty and integrity.

Third, they had to adhere to the Biblical standard of selflessness. They had to be men of impeccability, hating covetousness.

But, besides these prerequisites, they had to be men of ability as well. They had to adhere to the Biblical standard of excellence.

This standard of excellence is illustrated in the lives of Joseph, Nehemiah, and Daniel, but it is rooted in the very character of God Himself.

The great God of excellence calls us to emulate Him. He calls us to be men and women of excellence.

Sadly, the Church in our day has failed to hear or heed this call.

If we are to reclaim the land, if we are to be salt and light, if we are appropriately to render unto Him all things, then obviously we will have to overcome our addiction to mediocrity and adhere to the Biblical standard of excellence.

And the sooner, the better.

Finally then, brethren, we urge and exhort in the Lord Jesus that you should abound more and more, just as you received from us how you ought to walk and to please God (1 Thessalonians 4:1).

*

7

HONORABLE OPPOSITION

> Then Saul took three thousand chosen men from all Israel, and
> went to seek David and his men on the Rocks of the Wild Goats.
> So he came to the sheepfolds by the road, where there was a cave;
> and Saul went in to attend to his needs. David and his men were
> staying in the recesses of the cave. Then the men of David said to
> him, "This is the day of which the Lord said to you, 'Behold, I will
> deliver your enemy into your hand, that you may do to him as it
> seems good to you.' " And David arose and secretly cut off a corner
> of Saul's robe. Now it happened afterward that David's heart trou-
> bled him because he had cut Saul's robe. And he said to his men,
> "The Lord forbid that I should do this thing to my master, the
> Lord's anointed, to stretch out my hand against him, seeing he is
> the anointed of the Lord." So David restrained his servants with
> these words, and did not allow them to rise against Saul. And Saul
> got up from the cave and went on his way. David also arose after-
> ward, went out of the cave, and called out to Saul, saying, "My
> lord the king!" And when Saul looked behind him, David stooped
> with his face to the earth, and bowed down (1 Samuel 24:2-8).

This was David's big chance. With one swift blow, he could
have ended it all. The pain and anguish of exile, the shame and
torment of flight could have been over forever, then and there. No
longer would he have to live out his days as a renegade, a wanderer, a refugee, an outcast, or a pariah. He could have claimed
Saul's crown and taken Saul's throne.

But he didn't.

David was an honorable man.

Though Saul had pitilessly pursued him seeking his life

speculative spectacularization. It protects us from having to do battle unprepared and unguarded.

Alertness means checking the facts, doing the footwork, laying the foundations, and counting the cost.

David knew that.

So should we.

> Therefore gird up the loins of your mind, be sober, and rest your hope fully upon the grace that is to be brought to you at the revelation of Jesus Christ; as obedient children, not conforming yourselves to the former lusts, as in your ignorance; but as He who called you is holy, you also be holy in all your conduct (1 Peter 1:13-15).

Be Steadfast in the Faith

In his dealings with Saul, David was not just alert, he was also steadfast (1 Corinthians 16:13). He never wavered. He held his ground. He was *faithful* to his calling in God.

Just as Josiah remained steadfast (2 Kings 22:2), just as Daniel was steadfast (Daniel 6:5-11), and just as Job (Job 23:11), Shadrach, Mechach, and Abednego (Daniel 3:18), Peter and John (Acts 4:19-20), and the Apostle Paul (Acts 20:24) were all steadfast, so David remained unmovable in his devotion to truth, justice, and righteousness (Psalm 119:105-112). It was his unswerving faith that enabled him to defeat Goliath (1 Samuel 17:45-49). It was his unswerving faith that enabled him to defeat the Philistines (1 Samuel 19:8). And it was his unswerving faith that enabled him *honorably* to withstand the opposition of Saul.

Like his alertness, this steadfastness was not a special character trait unique to David. On the contrary, he was simply submitting to the ethical standard for *all* of God's people:

> Yet the righteous will hold to his way, and he who has clean hands will be stronger and stronger (Job 17:9).

> Therefore, my beloved brethren, be steadfast, immovable, always abounding in the work of the Lord, knowing that your labor is not in vain in the Lord (1 Corinthians 15:58).

Stand fast therefore in the liberty by which Christ has made us free, and do not be entangled again with a yoke of bondage (Galatians 5:1).

Each of us is to be steadfast in the faith (2 Thessalonians 2:25). We are commanded to stand firm in the midst of suffering (1 Peter 5:9), in the face of strange teaching (Hebrews 13:9), and in times of trying circumstances (James 1:12). We are to be steadfast in good works (Galatians 6:9). We are to be steadfast in enduring love (Hosea 6:4). We are to be steadfast in our conduct (Philippians 1:27), in our decision making (1 Kings 18:21), and in our absolute fealty to the Lord (Proverbs 24:21).

Steadfastness in political action protects us from ideological bullies, both liberal and conservative, who pursue the ever shifting, ever changing whims of fallen men. But it also protects us from our own doublemindedness. It secures us against doubt.

Steadfastness means adhering to God's *standards*, upholding God's *statutes*, applying God's *principles*, and enforcing God's *decrees*.

David knew that.

So should we.

Therefore, my beloved and longed-for brethren, my joy and crown, so stand fast in the Lord, beloved (Philippians 4:1).

Be Brave

In his dealings with Saul, David was not just alert and steadfast, he was also brave (1 Corinthians 16:13). He was a man of valor. He demonstrated courage.

In the same way that Caleb stood fearlessly before the enemies of God (Joshua 14:12); in the same way that Jonathan exhibited great courage (1 Samuel 14:6); in the same way that Jael (Judges 4:18-22), Ezra (Ezra 5:11), Nehemiah (Nehemiah 6:11), Daniel (Daniel 6:10), Ezekiel (Ezekiel 3:8-9), and Esther (Esther 4:8, 16) showed undeterred bravery, so David was a man of unquestioned valor. When all of Israel trembled in cowardice and fear before Goliath (1 Samuel 17:24), David remained confident and fearless

(1 Samuel 17:32). He showed courage in his service in the king's court (1 Samuel 18:1-14), in battle against the Philistines (1 Samuel 18:20-30), as a fugitive from Saul (1 Samuel 23:1-29), and in his dying days (1 Kings 2:1-11). It was his courage that enabled him *honorably* to oppose the king.

Once again though, this courage was not a special character trait unique to David. On the contrary, he was simply submitting to the ethical standard for *all* of God's people:

> The wicked flee when no one pursues, but the righteous are bold as a lion (Proverbs 28:1).

> God is our refuge and strength, a very present help in trouble. Therefore we will not fear, though the earth be removed, and though the mountains be carried into the midst of the sea; though its waters roar and be troubled, though the mountains shake with its swelling (Psalm 46:1-3).

> For God has not given us a spirit of fear, but of power and of love and of a sound mind (2 Timothy 1:7).

Each of us is to be courageous, fearless, and brave (Isaiah 12:2). Because we know that God is sovereign, we are to be courageous (2 Chronicles 32:7). Because we know that God is ever present, we are to be courageous (Psalm 118:6). We are to be brave in the face of our enemies (Deuteronomy 31:6) and brave in the midst of chastisement (Job 5:17-24). We are to show valor in obedience to the Word of God (Joshua 23:6) and for the sake of His people (2 Samuel 10:12). In all our service to the Lord we are ever to be courageous (1 Chronicles 28:20), even when we are terrified (Psalm 91:5) or dismayed (Joshua 10:25).

Courage in political action protects us from weak-willed and godless men who exploit our people and abuse our resources in exchange for mere token rhetoric. But it also protects us from retreatism and neutralism.

Courage means standing against the tide, struggling for right to the bitter end, and investing our all-in-all for the cause of the Kingdom.

David knew that.

So should we.

Be strong and of good courage, for to this people you shall divide as an inheritance the land which I swore to their fathers to give them. Only be strong and very courageous, that you may observe to do according to all the law which Moses My servant commanded you; do not turn from it to the right hand or to the left, that you may prosper wherever you go (Joshua 1:6-7).

Be Strong

In all his dealings with Saul, David was mighty, stalwart, dynamic, and strong (1 Corinthians 16:13). He was not merely alert, steadfast, and brave, he was powerful and robust as well.

In the same way that Abraham was mighty (Genesis 14:14-17); in the same way that Jacob was mighty (Genesis 32:22-32); in the same way that Gideon (Judges 7:19-25), Samson (Judges 15:14-20), and Stephen (Acts 6:8) were mighty, so David exercised strength and power over his adversaries (1 Samuel 23:1-14). He was mighty in love (2 Samuel 9:1-13) and mighty in war (1 Samuel 23:1-14). He showed his strength at home (2 Samuel 8:15) and abroad (2 Samuel 8:13-14). He was powerful in good deeds (2 Samuel 9:7) and in holy vindication (2 Samuel 4:9-12). His was no weak-minded rebellion. It was his *strength* that enabled him *honorably* to oppose the king.

But, as was the case with his alertness, steadfastness, and courage, this strength was not a special character trait unique to David. On the contrary, he was simply submitting to the ethical standard for *all* of God's people:

And He said to me, "My grace is sufficient for you, for My strength is made perfect in weakness." Therefore most gladly I will rather boast in my infirmities, that the power of Christ may rest upon me. Therefore I take pleasure in infirmities, in reproaches, in needs, in persecutions, in distresses, for Christ's sake. For when I am weak, then I am strong (2 Corinthians 12:9-10).

He gives power to the weak, and to those who have no might He increases strength. Even the youths shall faint and be weary, and the young men shall utterly fall, but those who wait on the Lord shall renew their strength; they shall mount up with wings like eagles, they shall run and not be weary, they shall walk and not faint (Isaiah 40:29-31).

Finally, my brethren, be strong in the Lord and in the power of His might. Put on the whole armor of God, that you may be able to stand against the wiles of the devil. For we do not wrestle against flesh and blood, but against principalities, against powers, against the rulers of the darkness of this age, against spiritual hosts of wickedness in the heavenly places. Therefore take up the whole armor of God, that you may be able to withstand in the evil day, and having done all, to stand. Stand therefore, having girded your waist with truth, having put on the breastplate of righteousness, and having shod your feet with the preparation of the gospel of peace; above all, taking the shield of faith with which you will be able to quench all the fiery darts of the wicked one. And take the helmet of salvation, and the sword of the Spirit, which is the word of God (Ephesians 6:10-17).

Each of us is to be mighty, stalwart, dynamic and strong (2 Corinthians 10:3-6). God has not given us a spirit of weakness but of *power* (2 Timothy 1:7). The wicked cannot know this power (Matthew 22:29), but every believer is anointed with it (Luke 24:49). The Gospel comes in power (1 Thessalonians 1:5), the Kingdom comes in power (1 Corinthians 4:19), and salvation comes in power (Romans 1:16). We have been endowed with strength to witness (Acts 1:8), strength to labor (Colossians 1:29), strength, in fact, to do *all* things (Philippians 4:13). We have the strength of His might (Ephesians 1:19) and the strength of His grace (2 Timothy 2:1).

Strength in political action protects us against any and all those who might be inclined to take undue advantage of us. But it also protects us from half-hearted and indecisive vacillation before the enemies of the Kingdom. It protects us from frailty and impotence in the face of tough issues and difficult circumstances.

Strength means harnessing the power of Christ to confront and to captivate the powers and the principalities, the rulers of this fallen world.

David knew that.

So should we.

For this reason I bow my knees to the Father of our Lord Jesus Christ, from whom the whole family in heaven and earth is named, that He would grant you, according to the riches of His glory, to be strengthened with might through His Spirit in the inner man, that Christ may dwell in your hearts through faith; that you, being rooted and grounded in love, may be able to comprehend with all the saints what is the width and length and depth and height—to know the love of Christ which passes knowledge; that you may be filled with all the fullness of God. Now to Him who is able to do exceedingly abundantly above all that we ask or think, according to the power that works in us, to Him be glory in the church by Christ Jesus throughout all ages, world without end. Amen. (Ephesians 3:14-21).

Be Loving

In his dealings with Saul, David was not only alert, steadfast, brave, and strong, he was loving as well (1 Corinthians 16:14). He was respectful, tender hearted, affectionate, kind, and just.

Just as Moses was longsuffering in love (Exodus 32:31-32); just as Nehemiah was tenderhearted (Nehemiah 1:2-11); just as Jonathan (1 Samuel 18:1-3), Hosea (Hosea 2:6-20), the Good Samaritan (Luke 10:30-37), and Paul (Philippians 1:3-9) were marked by love, so David showed affection and kindness in all his affairs. He was respectful of Saul's position, authority, and office (1 Samuel 24:2-8). He was affectionate toward the king himself (1 Samuel 16:21-23), the king's daughter (1 Samuel 16:20-28), the king's son (1 Samuel 18:1), and the king's grandson (2 Samuel 9:1-13). He was concerned for Saul's honor (1 Samuel 18:17-18) and enforced his prestige (1 Samuel 24:6). It was his lovingkindness than enabled him *honorably* to oppose the king.

Again though, this abiding love was not a special character trait unique to David. On the contrary, he was simply submitting to the ethical standard for *all* of God's people:

Therefore, as the elect of God, holy and beloved, put on tender mercies, kindness, humbleness of mind, meekness, long-suffering; bearing with one another, and forgiving one another, if anyone has a complaint against another; even as Christ forgave you, so you also must do (Colossians 3:12-14).

O my God, I trust in You. Let me not be ashamed. Let not my enemies triumph over me. Indeed, let no one who waits on the Lord be ashamed (Psalm 25:2-3).

Conclusion

The seventh basic principle in the Biblical blueprint for political action is that we must pose an honorable opposition to the powers that be. Our politics must be *thoroughly ethical*.

If we do the right thing in the wrong way, we will not succeed, nor will we glorify the name of Christ.

We must oppose the enemies of the kingdom, but we must oppose them honorably. We must learn to fight fair. Like David, we must develop a pattern of righteous resistance.

We must be alert. It is essential that we be aware and informed.

We must be steadfast. Our convictions must be unmovable and unshakable.

We must be brave. Fear and trembling before men have no place in our agenda.

We must be strong. God has endowed us with His might. Now we must use it.

And we must be loving. A deep respect for authority, office, and influence must mark our every thought, word, and deed.

In short, the ethical standards we carry into the political sphere must go well beyond mere honesty and sincerity. It is not enough to know that God desires for us to be salt and light, reclaiming the land through uncompromising conviction and undeterred excellence. We must oppose the forces of darkness with patience and honor.

Summary

David could have easily killed King Saul and claimed the throne of Israel for himself.

But he didn't. He was an honorable man.

Like the honorable man the Apostle Paul describes (1 Corinthians 16:13-14), David demonstrated his honor in five ways.

First, he was alert. He was aware and informed.

Second, he was steadfast. His faith was unshakable.

Third, he was brave. His courage was evident at all times, on the field of battle and off.

Fourth, he was strong. He walked in the might and power of the Lord.

And fifth, he was loving. He respected Saul and held him in fond affection.

These five attributes of patience and honor were essential to David's great success. And they will certainly need to be a part of *our* work in the ministry of political action if we are to meet with similar success.

The *right* way to exercise our political mandate as ambassadors of the King is the *good* way.

Therefore, my beloved brethren, be steadfast, immovable, always abounding in the work of the Lord, knowing that your labor is not in vain in the Lord (1 Corinthians 15:58).

And do not turn aside; for then you would go after empty things which cannot profit or deliver, for they are nothing. For the Lord will not forsake His people, for His great name's sake, because it has pleased the Lord to make you His people. Only fear the Lord, and serve Him in truth with all your heart; for consider what great things He has done for you. But if you still do wickedly, you shall be swept away, both you and your king (1 Samuel 12:21-22, 24-25).

A stand like that can be costly though, and it nearly cost Daniel everything.

Think of it. He had power (Daniel 6:3). He had influence (Daniel 5:12). He had prominence (Daniel 5:14). But he risked it *all* for the sake of conscience.

A simple *compromise* would have preserved his power, influence, and prominence. But he *refused* to compromise.

He could have tried to work within the system. He could have tried to wait out the edict. He wouldn't have had to *deny* his faith, just keep it quiet for a while. He could have tried conciliation, accommodation, or negotiation. Why *waste* everything that he had gained over such a small matter? Why not just play along, attempting to do good as the opportunity presented itself?

Daniel *refused* to compromise, risking prison and even death. He refused for three reasons.

Loyalty to God

First, Daniel understood who *really* governs men and nations. He did not need to tremble before mere human edicts. God and God alone directs the ebb and flow of history:

The king's heart is in the hand of the Lord, like the rivers of water; He turns it wherever He wishes (Proverbs 21:1).

For I know that the Lord is great, and our Lord is above all gods. Whatever the Lord pleases He does, in heaven and in earth, in the seas and in all deep places (Psalm 135:5-6).

Daniel knew that the security of power, influence, and prominence depended solely upon his loyalty and obedience to God:

> See, I have set before you today life and good, death and evil, in that I command you today to love the Lord your God, to walk in His ways, and to keep His commandments, His statutes, and His judgments, that you may live and multiply; and the Lord your God will bless you in the land which you go to possess (Deuteronomy 30:15-16).

Daniel knew that he couldn't play dirty little political games. Compromise would have been self-defeating.

The Inevitability of Persecution

Second, Daniel understood the nature of his opposition. He knew that his enemies would not be satisfied with anything less than the assassination of his faith and the obliteration of his privilege. Compromise would have been fruitless. It wouldn't have accomplished anything more than a watering down of his message.

"All those who desire to live godly lives *will* be persecuted" (2 Timothy 3:12). There is no way around it. No amount of compromise can divert it. Persecution is inevitable.

Jesus explained this fact to His disciples saying,

> If the world hates you, you know that it hated Me before it hated you. If you were of the world, the world would love its own. Yet because you are not of the world, but I chose you out of the world, therefore the world hates you. Remember the Word that I said to you, "A servant is not greater than his master." If they persecuted Me, they will also persecute you. If they kept My Word, they will keep yours also (John 15:18-20).

Thus, no matter what concessions or accommodations Daniel would have made, his enemies would have continued their assaults against him. Compromise would have done little more than buy some time.

The Promise of Prison

Third, Daniel understood that "God causes all things to work together for good to those who love God, to those who are called according to His purpose" (Romans 8:28). By refusing to compromise, he was risking prison or even death. But he knew that prison and death would become *opportunities* under the sovereign direction of God Almighty.

Like Daniel, *Joseph* risked everything by refusing to compromise his obedience to God (Genesis 39:7-16). As a result, he was thrown into prison (Genesis 39:19-20). But God used that prison as the first stage of dominion. Before long, Joseph was raised up out of the depths to rule over the whole land (Genesis 41:37-45).

Similarly, *David* risked everything by refusing to compromise his obedience to God (1 Samuel 18:1-16). As a result, he was cast into exile (1 Samuel 19:11-18). But God used exile as the first stage of dominion. Before long, David was raised up out of the depths to rule over the whole land (2 Samuel 2:4).

The *early Christians* also risked everything by refusing to compromise their obedience to God (Acts 4:19-20). As a result, they were thrown into prison (Acts 5:19). But God used prison as the first stage of dominion. Before long they were raised up out of the depths to rule over the whole land (Acts 19:26).

This *pattern* of reaction—repression—resurrection runs all throughout the Bible. It underlies the stories of Esther (Esther 3:6-15; 8:1-17), Job (Job 1:13-22; 42:10-15), Jeremiah (Jeremiah 37:11-16; 39:11-12), Elijah (1 Kings 17:1-16; 18:20-46), Hosea (Hosea 1:2-9; 3:1-5), Micaiah (1 Kings 22:7-12; 24-40), and the Apostle Paul (Philippians 1:7; 3:8-16). Like Daniel, each of these heroes of the faith witnessed the *resurrection* power of Almighty God. Each of them saw the most difficult and oppressive circumstances transformed into glorious victory. Each of them went from death to life, from bondage to liberty, from prison to promise. Each of them mirrored and illuminated the Gospel:

> For I delivered to you first of all that which I also received: that Christ died for our sins according to the Scriptures, and that He

was buried, and that He rose again the third day according to the Scriptures (1 Corinthians 15:3-4).

Jesus refused to compromise (Luke 22:42; Philippians 2:5-8). As a result, He was thrown into the prison of the grave (Matthew 16:21). But God used that prison as the first stage of dominion. On the third day Jesus arose out of the depths to rule and reign over the whole land (Philippians 2:9-11). This is the essence of the Gospel.

So, Daniel's uncompromising stand was rooted in his understanding of God's absolute sovereignty and man's resolute opposition. But it was also rooted in the privilege of prison and the promise of resurrection. He could remain steadfast because he recognized the reaction—repression—resurrection pattern in his own experience and could therefore "walk by faith and not by sight" (2 Corinthians 5:7).

Steadfastness and Humility

The uncompromising stance of believers is often mistaken for prideful self-assurance. Because he understood who *really* governs men and nations, because he understood the nature of His opposition, and because he understood that God would transform prison into promise, Daniel refused to hedge God's statutes (Daniel 1:8; 6:5). His enemies took this to be mere hardheaded stubbornness (Daniel 6:13). They presumed that Daniel was just another in a long line of self-confident, egotistical, and dogmatic bureaucrats—a prideful, pompous, and pertinacious Persian political pretender!

Joseph's enemies thought the same thing (Genesis 37:8). They assumed that he was a swaggering, self-promoting braggart—an irascible, irrational, and intractable inferno of indomitable indolence!

Virtually all of God's heroes through time have been accused of having a self-indulgent, self-inflating, and self-assuming attitude: Moses (Ezekiel 2:14), Job (Job 8:2), David (1 Samuel 18:8), and even Jesus (Matthew 9:3). Uncompromising steadfastness is almost always confused with unreasoning pontification. Righteousness is thus labeled "intolerance," and righteous men and women are popularly diagnosed as "suffering from delusions of grandeur."

But nothing could be further from the truth.

Uncompromising believers throughout the ages who have "conquered kingdoms, performed acts of righteousness, obtained promises, shut the mouths of lions, quenched the power of fire, escaped the edge of the sword, and from weakness were made strong," did so *"by faith"* (Hebrews 11:33-34). In other words, they trusted *God* rather than themselves. Far from having confidence or certainty in their *own* flesh, their *own* ideas, their *own* understanding, their *own* abilities, their *own* strength, and their *own* ingenuity, they put their full reliance on God (Philippians 3:3). They obtained victory even amidst travail, not because they were domineeringly proud, but because they were submissively humble (Matthew 5:3-12).

The Bible is crystal clear in this matter:

> Rest in the Lord, and wait patiently for Him; do not fret because of him who prospers in his way, because of the man who brings wicked schemes to pass. Cease from anger, and forsake wrath; do not fret—it only causes harm. For evildoers shall be cut off; but those who wait on the Lord, they shall inherit the earth. For yet a little while and the wicked shall be no more; indeed, you will look diligently for his place, but it shall be no more. But the meek shall inherit the earth, and shall delight themselves in the abundance of peace (Psalm 37:7-11).

> The fear of the Lord is the instruction of wisdom, and before honor is humility (Proverbs 15:33).

> Before destruction the heart of a man is haughty, and before honor is humility (Proverbs 18:12).

> By humility and the fear of the Lord are riches and honor and life (Proverbs 22:4).

> But Jesus called them to Himself and said, "You know that the rulers of the Gentiles lord it over them, and those who are great exercise authority over them. Yet it shall not be so among you but whoever desires to become great among you, let him be your servant. And whoever desires to be first among you, let him be your

slave—just as the Son of Man did not come to be served, but to serve, and to give His life a ransom for many" (Matthew 20:25-28).

Thus the reason Daniel was able to square off against the forces of evil without compromise involved not only what he *knew*, but what he *was*. And *he was humble*. His steadfastness was not closed-minded obstinacy. Instead, his understanding of absolute sovereignty, persistent opposition, and the promise of prison was rooted in *a true humility*.

The fact is Daniel *couldn't* have done what he was able to do had he not been humble, no matter how well he understood the situations and circumstances swirling about him.

Living by faith, walking in steadfastness, and partaking of resurrection power is completely and entirely dependent on righteous humility. Recognizing and prospering amidst the reaction— repression—resurrection pattern is utterly impossible apart from godly meekness.

Hope from Prison

The Apostle Paul emphasized this truth when he wrote to the besieged believers in Philippi. He reminded them that their stand for the Gospel had to remain absolutely uncompromised, but in doing so he outlined in broad brush strokes the Biblical reaction— repression—resurrection pattern; he reminded them that it is God who *really* rules men and nations (Philippians 1:12-26), and he reminded them that prison is the first stage of dominion (Philippians 1:1-11).

Once he had stated the *necessity* for steadfastness, he reiterated that humility is the *only* means to attain to that steadfastness. The Philippians were not to have any confidence in their own flesh (Philippians 3:1-7). On the contrary, they were to imitate the Lord Jesus:

> Let this mind be in you which was also in Christ Jesus, who, being in the form of God, did not consider it robbery to be equal with God, but made Himself of no reputation, taking the form of a servant, and coming in the likeness of men. And being found in

appearance as a man, He humbled Himself and became obedient to the point of death, even the death of the cross. Therefore God also has highly exalted Him and given Him the name which is above every name, that at the name of Jesus every knee should bow, of those in heaven, and of those on earth, and of those under the earth, and that every tongue should confess that Jesus Christ is Lord, to the glory of God the Father (Philippians 2:5-11).

They were also to imitate the Apostle Paul (Philippians 3:17) who asserted:

> But indeed I also count all things loss for the excellence of the knowledge of Christ Jesus my Lord, for whom I have suffered the loss of all things, and count them as rubbish, that I may gain Christ and be found in Him, not having my own righteousness, which is from the law, but that which is through faith in Christ, the righteousness which is from God by faith; that I may know Him and the power of His resurrection, and the fellowship of His sufferings, being conformed to His death, if, by any means, I may attain to the resurrection from the dead (Philippians 3:8-11).

Believers can stand firm on the truth despite opposition and persecution. We can emerge victorious, transforming prison into promise. We can know the power of Christ's resurrection.

But only if we are humble.

We cannot hope to win the battle for the hearts of men and the souls of nations if we constantly compromise Biblical essentials (Matthew 28:20). But then, neither can we hope to win that battle if we carry airs of superiority (Matthew 5:3-5).

The Religious Right

You might automatically assume that the emergence of the religious right as a major force in American politics is cause for great joy. And in many respects it is.

Certainly, steadfastness has been manifested. The religious right has been thrown into a media lion's den of criticism and persecution, yet it continues to stand for Scriptural values. It continues to prick the American conscience and sway the American consensus.

Even so, the dirty little game of politics makes for strange bed-fellows. All too often naive, inexperienced, and uninitiated, the religious right often found itself allied with the old line traditionalists and conservatives. And it found itself being used. It found itself yoked together with Belial (2 Corinthians 6:14-18). Rushing headlong into established partisan politics, Christians failed to recognize until late in the game that a conservative humanism is little better than a liberal humanism. By exchanging yippies for yuppies, Democrats for Republicans, and Modernists for traditionalists, the religious right did little more than domesticate its own steadfastness. It wound up compromised by default.

If the religious right is ever to accomplish its stated goal of returning our nation to moral sanity and spiritual stability, it must humbly but determinedly *set its own course* according to the wind of the Spirit of God. It must no longer be the pawn of powers and principalities, of godless men and institutions be they left or right.

In short, the religious right must not compromise—even in its pose of humble steadfastness!

We must be uncompromising. But we must also be humble. We must meet the challenge of politics with the same commitment to Biblical surety that we convey in every other sphere of life and godliness. We must "speak boldly" (Titus 3:8), "confidently" (Ephesians 6:20), and "without fear" (Philippians 1:14). But we must speak the truth *in love* (Ephesians 4:15).

Conclusion

The eighth basic principle in the Biblical blueprint for political action is that we must not compromise. But, that steadfastness must be marked by humility.

Like Daniel, we owe our full allegiance to God Almighty. We must not—we can not—waffle when God's purposes are at issue.

There can be *no compromise* on the sanctity of human life. Abortion *must* be stopped. Infanticide *must* be stopped. Euthanasia *must* be stopped. This *must* be an absolute priority for anyone called by God into the ministry of political action. This *must* be an absolute priority for every other Christian citizen as well. There are no "ifs," "buts," or "ands" about it—regardless of the risk to our power, influence, and prominence. (See my book, *Lifelight: The Bible and the Sanctity of Human Life* [Ft. Worth, Texas: Dominion Press, 1987].)

There can be *no compromise* on ethics and morality. A conservative humanism is no better than a liberal humanism. Man-centered values—whether from the left or the right, whether traditional or contemporary—*must* be eliminated from our cultural and political ecology. We must stand steadfastly on the Word of God as our *only* guide to truth and life.

Similarly, there can be *no compromise* on the integrity of the family, the freedom of commerce and enterprise, the limitation of federal intervention, regulation, and taxation, the diligent care of the poor and distressed, the autonomy and liberty of the Church, etc. In each of these areas, we *must* stand steadfast. God's decrees dare not be compromised.

We must recognize, as Daniel did, that God is sovereign, that opposition is inevitable, and that even the worst persecution offers with it promise and privilege. If we do, then we will not fear. The reaction—repression—resurrection pattern in Scripture gives us the assurance that an uncompromising stand will ultimately be blessed and used by God.

But—our steadfastness must be rooted in humility. Our uncompromising commitment must not rest on self-confidence and self-assurance, but on confidence in God and the assurance that comes by trusting in His "very great and precious promises" (2 Peter 1:3).

Only when we stand, like Daniel, uncompromisingly yet humbly, can we hope to avoid the dirty games and sordid ploys of the political process.

Summary

Daniel refused to play the game of politics. He was uncompromising in his commitment to God. He was unyielding in his godly convictions. And thus, he risked all the power, influence, and privilege that he had.

He was willing to risk that power, influence, and privilege because:

First, he understood who *really* governs men and nations. *God* is sovereign and thus the risks of uncompromising faithfulness are more than balanced out by the benefits.

Second, he understood that opposition was inevitable. To compromise would not have appeased Daniel's enemies. Better to keep his message undiluted and face the risks than to compromise and *still* be under the fires of persecution.

Third, he understood that God would transform persecution into promise. Prison is the first stage of dominion, so an uncompromising stand is worth the risk. Risk offers resurrection.

This reaction—repression—resurrection pattern is not only evident in Daniel's life, it appears throughout the Scriptures providing for us the security we need to imitate the heroes of the faith.

But imitating unwavering steadfastness is not all we must do in order to procure victory. We must root our uncompromising posture in humility as well.

Our confidence must be in God. Our own ingenuity, our own skillfulness, and our own willfulness is not sufficient or satisfactory. We must yield to Him. We must be uncompromising. But we must also be humble.

In short, we must unswervingly speak the truth. But we must speak that truth with true, loving kindness.

He knew that ultimately he would have to exercise his political options. He knew that he would have to win the king's favor (Nehemiah 1:11), obtain the king's blessing (Nehemiah 2:1-5), and utilize the king's resources (Nehemiah 2:6-9).

But for now, he *just* prayed.

For an entire month he prayed (Nehemiah 1:1; 2:1).

His response to the political crisis in Jerusalem speaks volumes for his character and for the character of his faith. He understood clearly the consequences of sin (Jeremiah 14:1-22). He had a good grasp of the dynamics of history (Job 42:1-2). He showed a thorough understanding of divine providence (Proverbs 21:1). He obviously understood the multi-generational nature of the kingdom task (Lamentations 5:19). He displayed a keen awareness of the *power of prayer* (2 Chronicles 7:13-14). His response gives testimony to his utter *dependence* upon God, and his confidence in Biblical problem solving (Psalm 34:17-18). He wanted to do things God's way, in God's time, with God's help, in accord with God's will.

So, he prayed.

The Life of Prayer

Prayer is an essential element in *any* program of change. This is what Jesus was trying to teach His disciples. This is what Nehemiah was trying to convey to his constituency. If we want to change our nation politically, or any other way, then we must pray. The solution to our grave moral, economic, cultural, sociological, and civil dilemmas cannot and will not be achieved without prayer.

Prayer changes things.

That is why the Scriptures are brimming over with exhortations to be *constant* in prayer.

Oh, give thanks to the Lord! Call upon His name; make known His deeds among the peoples! Sing to Him, sing psalms to Him; talk of all His wondrous works! Glory in His holy name; let the hearts of those rejoice who seek the Lord! Seek the Lord and His strength; seek His face evermore! (1 Chronicles 16:8-11).

Ask, and it will be given to you; seek, and you will find; knock, and it will be opened to you (Matthew 7:7).

Watch and pray, lest you enter into temptation. The spirit indeed is willing, but the flesh is weak (Matthew 26:41).

Watch therefore, and pray always that you may be counted worthy to escape all these things that will come to pass, and to stand before the Son of Man (Luke 21:36).

. . . praying always with all prayer and supplication in the Spirit, being watchful to this end with all perseverance and supplication for all the saints (Ephesians 6:18).

We are to pray.

We are to pray with wholeheartedness (Jeremiah 29:13). We are to pray with contrition (2 Chronicles 7:14). We are to pray with all faith (Mark 11:24). We are to pray with righteous fervor (James 5:16). We are to pray out of obedience (1 John 3:22) and with full confidence (John 15:7). We are to pray in the morning (Mark 1:35), and in the evening (Mark 6:46), during the night watch (Luke 6:12), and at all other times (1 Thessalonians 5:17).

God has given us access to His throne (Hebrews 4:16) and fellowship with Christ (1 Corinthians 1:9). And He expects us to make use of that glorious privilege at *every* opportunity (1 Timothy 2:8).

Nehemiah did.

At every turn, Nehemiah made supplication to the Lord God on high. When he appeared before Artaxerxes to make petition to rebuild the walls of Jerusalem, *he prayed* (Nehemiah 2:4). When he entered the ruined city to begin the task, *he prayed* (Nehemiah 2:12). When threats of violence and conspiracy jeopardized the fledgling reconstruction project, *he prayed* (Nehemiah 4:2). When there were conflicts and crises among the people that required his judicious hand, first *he prayed* (Nehemiah 5:19). When an attempt on his life threatened the entire project, he didn't panic—*he prayed* (Nehemiah 6:9). When his own brethren turned against him, *he prayed* (Nehemiah 6:14). And when the work on the walls was complete—you might have guessed it—*he prayed* (Nehemiah 13:31).

Nehemiah's whole political platform was built on prayer.

The Foundation of Political Action

Of course, praying wasn't *all* that he did. But it was the *foundation* of all that he did. Like anyone called by God into the ministry of political action, he invested himself in careful planning (Nehemiah 2:5-6). He laid the groundwork with cautious attention to detail (Nehemiah 2:7-8). He enlisted qualified help (Nehemiah 2:9). He encouraged his workers (Nehemiah 2:17-18). He motivated them (Nehemiah 4:14-20). He organized and delegated the various tasks (Nehemiah 3:1-32). He anticipated difficulty and made provision for it (Nehemiah 2:19-20; 6:1-14). He improvised, when he had to (Nehemiah 4:21-23), and worked (Nehemiah 4:23). He sacrificed (Nehemiah 5:14-19), led (Nehemiah 13:4-30), and governed (Nehemiah 7:1-7). But undergirding all these necessary political activities was his *constant* reliance upon Almighty God. Undergirding them all was *prayer*.

Nehemiah knew that it is pointless to attempt *anything* apart from God's blessing and purpose:

> Unless the Lord builds the house, they labor in vain who build it; unless the Lord guards the city, the watchman stays awake in vain. It is vain for you to rise up early, to sit up late, to eat the bread of sorrows; for so He gives His beloved sleep (Psalm 127:1-2).

The prayer life of Nehemiah indicated that he wanted, more than anything else, to do God's will. He wanted to be accountable—accountable for his actions, for his intentions, and for the fruit of his labor.

He didn't want God to simply "okay" *his* plans. He wanted to do what *God* wanted him to do.

Prayer held him accountable to that. It gave him the resolve to *stick* to that. Prayer gave him access to God's will, God's way, God's purposes, and God's plan.

Nehemiah was confident that God would give him success (Nehemiah 2:20). He was sure God would give him strength (Nehemiah 6:9), show him favor (Nehemiah 2:18), and see him through (Nehemiah 2:12). He was unwavering in his optimism because the work was conceived *by* God, not by him (Nehemiah 7:5). It was *God's* project, *not* his.

Thus, it is clear that Nehemiah didn't pray in order to *get* something. He prayed in order to *be* something (James 4:3). He wanted to *be* conformed to God's will. He wanted to *be* used in God's work. He wanted to *be* obedient.

And his life of prayer enabled him to *be* those things.

The Priority of Prayer

Nehemiah was not unique.

All throughout the Scriptures the priority of prayer is more than evident in the lives and ministries of God's world-changers. Abraham was a man of prayer (Genesis 15:1-21). Joseph was a godly man who feared the Lord, seeking Him in prayer (Genesis 42:18). Moses, too, was constant in his fellowship with God (Numbers 14:11-38). Likewise, Joshua (Joshua 7:6-15), Gideon (Judges 6:36-40), Samuel (1 Samuel 12:23), David (Psalm 5:1-3), Solomon (1 Kings 8:22-53), Elijah (1 Kings 18:36-37), Asaph (Psalm 73:1-28), Jeremiah (Jeremiah 14:1-9), Daniel (Daniel 6:10), and a whole host of others were first and foremost men and women of prayer.

When Jesus sat his disciples down to teach them to pray, they already knew all this. So, the Lord was merely reinforcing the pattern already established by Nehemiah and the others. He was merely reinforcing the foundational truth that *prayer changes things*.

It binds and it looses (Matthew 18:18). It casts down and it raises up (Mark 11:23-24). It ushers in peace (1 Timothy 2:1-2), forgiveness (Mark 11:25), healing (James 5:14-15), liberty (2 Corinthians 3:17), wisdom (1 Kings 3:3-14), and protection (Psalm 41:2). Clearly, "the effective fervent prayer of a righteous man avails much" (James 5:16).

An Objective Standard

Prayer and politics!

What an odd combination! It sounds so esoteric. It sounds so otherworldly. And worst of all, it sounds so subjective.

What is to keep a Christian magistrate from "hearing voices from heaven" to, say, annihilate half the world one madcap evening? What limits can we possibly hope to impose on someone who can always appeal to a "higher authority?" What is to keep us from turning politics into a springboard for a whole host of petty tyrants all claiming the authority and anointing of an Ayatollah?

The answer of course is that Christian prayer is hedged by the immutable rampart of the *Biblical* covenant. It is rooted in an objective, unchanging standard.

That standard is the Word of God. It is the Bible.

Notice that Nehemiah's prayer life led him directly to *the* covenantal blueprint, *the* covenantal standard, *the* covenantal precept that underlies *all* things: the Bible. He prayed because he desired to do only the will of God. And because the Bible is the written and revealed will of God, it was only natural that Nehemiah's prayer life would be inextricably tied to Scripture.

Nehemiah made certain that God's Law took a very prominent place in the life of the people (Nehemiah 8:1-8). He encouraged its reading (Nehemiah 8:18), its exposition (Nehemiah 8:13), and its application (Nehemiah 8:14-18). He established it as the absolute standard for worship (Nehemiah 13:10-14), for commerce (Nehemiah 13:15-18), for governance (Nehemiah 13:4-9), for administering justice (Nehemiah 13:19-22), and for family life (Nehemiah 13:23-29).

He knew that to conform himself to God's will, he could not simply toss up a few prayers heavenward. He knew he would have to confirm his prayer life by the objective standard of the eternal, established Word of Truth (Psalm 119:152).

> Seek the Lord while He may be found, call upon Him while He is near. Let the wicked forsake his way, and the unrighteous man his thoughts; let him return to the Lord, and He will have mercy on him; and to our God, for He will abundantly pardon.
>
> "For My thoughts are not your thoughts, nor are your ways My ways," says the Lord. For as the heavens are higher than the earth, so are My ways higher than your ways, and My thoughts than your thoughts. For as the rain comes down, and the snow from heaven, and do not return there, but water the earth, and make it bring forth and bud, that it may give seed to the sower and

bread to the eater, so shall My word be that goes forth from My mouth; it shall not return to Me void, but it shall accomplish what I please, and it shall prosper in the thing for which I sent it. For you shall go out with joy, and be led out with peace; the mountains and the hills shall break forth into singing before you, and all the trees of the field shall clap their hands. Instead of the thorn shall come up the cypress tree, and instead of the brier shall come up the myrtle tree; and it shall be to the Lord for a name, for an everlasting sign that shall not be cut off (Isaiah 55:6-13).

We must seek God in prayer. But because our thoughts are not His thoughts, and our ways are not His ways, we need to have the Word of God guide and direct us. It must be our only rule, our final appeal for all matters, in life and godliness.

Nehemiah understood that all too *well*.

He prayed so that in all his *doing* he might not fall into any error. He studied the Word so that in all his *praying* he might not fall into any error, either. Only the Word can protect us from such error (Matthew 22:29). Only the Word can give perfect and objective guidance into all truth (Psalm 119:160), for it is a lamp to the feet and a light to the path (Psalm 119:105). Only the Word can keep us within covenant confines (1 Corinthians 4:6).

Diligence in prayer, thus, *must* be accomplished by a dependence on the Bible.

This Book of the Law shall not depart from your mouth, but you shall meditate in it day and night, that you may observe to do according to all that is written in it. For then you will make your way prosperous, and then you will have good success (Joshua 1:8).

All Scripture is given by inspiration of God, and is profitable for doctrine, for reproof, for correction, for instruction in righteousness, that the man of God may be complete, thoroughly equipped for every good work (2 Timothy 3:16-17).

We also have the prophetic word made more sure, which you do well to heed as a light that shines in a dark place, until the day dawns and the morning star rises in your hearts; knowing this first, that no prophecy of Scripture is of any private interpretation, for prophecy never came by the will of man, but holy men of God spoke as they were moved by the Holy Spirit (2 Peter 1:19-21).

Biblical prayer is rooted in the *objective* Word of God. It is grounded in the unchanging standard of the Bible.

If we are going to see the reign and rule of Christ manifested on earth as it is in heaven, we must pray. And if we are to pray properly, it must be rooted in God's precepts.

Prayer and precept in politics. Such is the way of the called of God.

10

FACING THE ODDS

Moreover, brethren, I do not want you to be unaware that all
our fathers were under the cloud, all passed through the sea, all
were baptized into Moses in the cloud and in the sea, all ate the
same spiritual food, and all drank the same spiritual drink. For
they drank of that spiritual Rock that followed them, and that
Rock was Christ. But with most of them God was not well pleased,
for their bodies were scattered in the wilderness. Now these things
became our examples, to the intent that we should not lust after
evil things as they also lusted. And do not become idolaters as were
some of them. As it is written, "The people sat down to eat and
drink, and rose up to play." Nor let us commit sexual immorality,
as some them did, and in one day twenty-three thousand fell; nor let
us tempt Christ, as some of them also tempted, and were destroyed
by serpents; nor murmur, as some of them also murmured, and
were destroyed by the destroyer. Now all these things happened to
them as examples, and they were written for our admonition, on
whom the ends of the ages have come (1 Corinthians 10:1-11).

God has set before us examples. Examples of victory. Examples of defeat. Examples of righteousness. Examples of debauchery. Good examples and bad examples.

God has set them before us for our instruction. He wants us to
learn some important lessons. He wants us to hear and heed.

We are to *imitate* those who walked before us in holiness and
truth. We are to *avoid* the mistakes of those who walked before us
in wickedness. The great heroes of the faith are to be our *models*
for godly living (Hebrews 12:1). The great villains are to be our
warnings (1 Corinthians 15:33).

101

This is in fact the essence of discipleship: *following the example of those righteous men and women who have gone before us, shunning the example of the wicked.*

That is why the Apostle Paul was *so* insistent that his converts imitate him (1 Corinthians 4:6; 11:1) and follow his example (Philippians 3:17; 4:9; 1 Thessalonians 1:6; 2 Thessalonians 3:9). And it is why Christ was constantly exhorting the believers to follow in His footsteps (1 Peter 2:21), to come after him (Matthew 16:24), to take up His yoke (Matthew 11:29), to fix their thoughts (Hebrews 3:1) and their eyes (Hebrews 12:2) on Him.

Discipleship is imitative (1 Timothy 4:12). We learn what to do and how to do it by following those who have walked the pilgrim's pathway ahead of us. They provide for us a pattern, a precedent, a kind of hands-on training program for dominion.

They also provide for us very real encouragement.

God's Word can be trusted. His promises are certain. Our inheritance is secure. The victory is ours, even when we're standing against all odds.

How can we be so sure?

Because God has set before us examples. He has demonstrated His faithfulness in the lives of those who have gone before We can have confidence in the future because we have seen His mighty acts in the past (Revelation 15:3-4).

God has given us His Word.

And He has matched Word with deed.

On such is faith established.

> Now faith is the substance of things hoped for, the evidence of things not seen. For by it the elders obtained a good testimony (Hebrews 11:1-2).

Against all odds, against all hope, they obtained victory. They snatched glory out of the jaws of despair. They hurdled insurmountable obstacles to "lay hold" of the good things of the Lord (Hebrews 6:18). By faith they believed God for the remarkable, for the impossible (Matthew 19:26; Hebrews 11:1-40). By faith they "subdued kingdoms, worked righteousness, obtained promises, stopped the mouths of lions, quenched the edge of the sword, out of weakness were made strong, became valiant in battle, turned to flight the armies of the aliens" (Hebrews 11:33-34). Though they were mocked and persecuted, imprisoned and tortured, impoverished and dispossessed, they were unshaken and eventually obtained God's great reward (Hebrews 11:35-40).

And God has set these before us as examples: Abraham (Genesis 12:1-4), Sarah (Genesis 18:11-14), Isaac (Genesis 27:27-29), Jacob (Genesis 48:1-20), Joseph (Genesis 50:24-26), Moses (Exodus 14:22-29), Rahab (Joshua 6:23), Ruth (Ruth 1:16-17), Gideon (Judges 6:1-8:35), Barak (Judges 4:1-5:31), Samson (Judges 13:1-16:31), Jephthah (Judges 11:1-12:7), David (1 Samuel 16:1-17:58), Isaiah (Isaiah 1:1-6:13), Samuel, and all the prophets (1 Samuel 1:1-28; Hebrews 11:32).

> Therefore we also, since we are surrounded by so great a cloud of witnesses, let us lay aside every weight, and the sin which so easily ensnares us, and let us run with endurance, the race that is set before us, looking unto Jesus, the author and finisher of our faith, who for the joy that was set before Him endured the cross, despising the shame, and has sat down at the right hand of the throne of God (Hebrews 12:1-2).

By their example we can be and should be assured that we are more than conquerors (Romans 8:37), overcomers (1 John 5:4), and victorious in Christ (1 Corinthians 15:57). By their example we can be and should be assured that *the future is ours.*

Avoiding Mistakes

When Israel went up after the exodus to take possession of the land, they too had examples of encouragement set before them.

They were very well aware of what God had *said.* They *knew* His promises. They knew that the land was theirs for the taking (Genesis 12:1-3), that it belonged to God, *not* to the Canaanites (Psalm 24:1), and that God had entrusted it into *their* care (Joshua 1:2). They knew that if only they would obey God's Word and do God's work, they would be prosperous and successful (Joshua

1:8), that every place which the soles of their feet trod would be granted to them (Joshua 1:3), and that no man would be able to stand before them all the days of their lives (Joshua 1:5).

They *knew* that.

They also knew that God had *already* confirmed the authority and veracity of His Word.

Sure there were "giants in the land" (Numbers 13:33). But there was no need to fear them. The giants had already been beaten. The examples were set before the people throughout Bible history. Time and time again, the sons of Shem had demonstrated that even giants were no match for a people with the blessing of God.

The great Shemite king Chedorlaomer (Genesis 10:22; 14:1) and his Japhethite allies (Genesis 9:25-27; 14:1) had no trouble whatsoever subduing the giants: He conquered "the Rephaim in Ashteroth Karnaim, the Zuzim in Ham, the Emim in Shaveh Kiriathaim, and the Horites in their mountain of Seir, as far as El Paran, which is by the wilderness. Then he turned back and came to En Mishpat (that is, Kadesh), and conquered all the country of the Amalekites, and also the Amorites who dwelt in Hazezon Tamar" (Genesis 14:5-7).

And following Chedorlaomer's romp, his Shemite cousin, Abraham, turned right around and defeated *him* (Genesis 14:13-17). Thus was fulfilled *both* Noah's prophecy that the Canaanites would be "the servants of servants" (Genesis 9:25) and God's covenant promise that all the land of Canaan would be Abraham's (Genesis 15:18-21).

Israel's Shemite brethren, the Moabites and the Ammonites, also had taken dominion over the fierce Rephaim, the Emim, the Anakim, the Zamzummin, and all the other giants (Deuteronomy 2:9-12, 19-23).

The fact is, Shemites had *always* been giant killers! Such examples spoke for themselves.

Thus, Israel had *nothing* to fear from the giants. God had *proven* that, in Word and in deed. He had set before them examples. He showed them their victory ahead of time. All they had to do was to imitate the righteous.

But they refused to hear or heed.

All the enemies that they feared: the Rephaim, the Anakim, the Amalekites, the Hittites, the Jebusites, the Nephilim, and all the other sons of Ham had already been defeated many times over (Numbers 13:28-29, 33). They were *far* from invincible.

But the Israelites would have none of that. They were obsessed with the odds. They trembled at the sight of the giants, forgetting their Shemite giant-killing heritage altogether (Numbers 13:29-33).

They ignored God's Word. They denied God's work. They spurned God's examples of encouragement, and so they were defeated (Numbers 14:40-45).

As we venture into the arena of political action to face the humanist Rephaim, Anakim, and Zamzummin of our own day, it would stand us in good stead to recall these lessons. If we are to survive, much less to win, we must learn from the examples God has set before us. We must face the odds with faith.

In Spite of it All

We are invincible (Ephesians 6:10-18; Romans 8:37-39). Even the gates of hell cannot prevail against us (Matthew 16:8). *If,* that is, we would only do our job. *If* we would only "make disciples of all the nations." *If* we would only "occupy till He comes" (Luke 19:13). If we would only pay heed to the examples God has set before us (1 Corinthians 10:6, 11).

God has given us the victory already (1 Corinthians 15:57).

All we have to do is go forth with diligence and claim it (Genesis 1:28).

We may have to work with few or even no resources at first, like David (1 Samuel 17:38-40) or Jonathan (1 Samuel 14:6).

We may have to improvise, utilizing less than perfect conditions and less than qualified workers and less than adequate facilities, like Aaron (Exodus 25:1-29:46) or Nehemiah (Nehemiah 1:20).

We may have to battle the powers that be, the rulers and the principalities, like Deborah (Judges 4:4-24) or Peter, James, and John (Acts 4:17-20).

We may have to go with what we've got, with virtually no support, no notoriety, and no cooperation, like Elijah (1 Kings 19:1-18) or Jeremiah (Jeremiah 1:4-10).

We may have to start "in weakness, in fear, and in much trembling" (1 Corinthians 2:3), without "persuasive words of wisdom" (1 Corinthians 2:4), like the Apostle Paul (1 Corinthians 2:1) or Moses (Exodus 4:1-17).

Instead of allowing their limitations and liabilities to discourage and debilitate them, the heroes of the faith went to work. God's power was made manifest in their weakness (1 Corinthians 1:26-29). In spite of the odds, they won. By faith.

And God has set them before us as examples.

Against all odds, Ehud faced the power of Moab and won (Judges 3:12-30). Against all odds, Shamgar faced the power of the Philistines and won (Judges 3:31). Against all odds, Gideon faced the power of Midian and won (Judges 6:12-8:35). Against all odds, David faced the power of Goliath and won (1 Samuel 17:42-52). Against all odds, Jonathan faced the power of the Canaanites and won (1 Samuel 14:1-15).

Against all odds, God gave His faithful people victory. Against all odds, He made them examples for us.

Isn't it high time for us to imitate them, to follow in their footsteps, to pay heed to their example? Isn't it high time for us to demonstrate to an unbelieving world that God can *still* beat the odds? Isn't it high time for us to prove to a fallen and depraved generation that God can raise up a weak and unesteemed people against all odds and win? Isn't it high time for a changing of the guard? Isn't it?

Covenant Blessings

In the heart of the Pentateuch, God lists the covenant blessings that He will shower upon any society that is faithful to Him and His Word:

> Now it shall come to pass, if you diligently obey the voice of the Lord your God, to observe carefully all His commandments which I command you today, that the Lord your God will set you high above all nations of the earth. And all these blessings shall come

upon you and overtake you, because you obey the voice of the Lord your God: "Blessed shall you be in the city, and blessed shall you be in the country. Blessed shall be the fruit of your body, the produce of your ground and the increase of your herds, the increase of your cattle and the offspring of your flocks. Blessed shall be your basket and your kneading bowl. Blessed shall you be when you come in, and blessed shall you be when you go out. The Lord will cause your enemies who rise against you to be defeated before your face; they shall come out against you one way and flee before you seven ways. The Lord will command the blessing on you in your storehouses and in all to which you set your hand, and He will bless you in the land which the Lord your God is giving you. The Lord will establish you as a holy people to Himself, just as He has sworn to you, if you keep the commandments of the Lord your God and walk in His ways. Then all peoples of the earth shall see that you are called by the name of the Lord, and they shall be afraid of you. And the Lord will grant you plenty of goods, in the fruit of your body, in the increase of your livestock, and in the produce of your ground, in the land which the Lord swore to your fathers to give you. The Lord will open to you His good treasure, the heavens, to give the rain to your land in its season, and to bless all the work of your hand. You shall lend to many nations, but you shall not borrow. And the Lord will make you the head and not the tail; you shall be above only, and not be beneath, if you heed the commandments of the Lord your God, which I command you today, and are careful to observe them. So you shall not turn aside from any of the words which I command you this day, to the right hand or to the left, to go after other gods to serve them" (Deuteronomy 28:1-14).

How could any Christian walk away from these blessings? How could any Christian seriously believe that none of this can happen in history, now that Satan's defeat at Calvary is behind us?

Conclusion

The tenth basic principle of the Biblical blueprint for political action is that we can face the odds . . . and win. We have God's sure Word. We have the evidence of His mighty acts throughout history. We *can* do it!

To be sure, the odds are stacked against us. Even so, God has assured us the victory is ours for the taking.

The road to victory may be fraught with danger and difficulty. But the Lord will clear the way. He has promised us He would.

We need only to follow the example of the righteous men and women who have gone before us. We need only to imitate those who have taken God at His Word, facing the odds and claiming dominion.

If we are salt and light, reclaiming the land with excellence, valor, and honor, no force on the face of this earth will be able to withstand us. Nothing will be withheld from us.

> For though we walk in the flesh, we do not war according to the flesh. For the weapons of our warfare are not carnal but mighty in God for pulling down strongholds, casting down arguments and every high thing that exalts itself against the knowledge of God, bringing every thought into captivity to the obedience of Christ, and being ready to punish all disobedience when your obedience is fulfilled (2 Corinthians 10:3-6).

Against all odds, we *can* win. Against all odds, we *shall* win.

Summary

God has set before us examples: good examples to imitate, bad examples to avoid.

This is, in fact, the essence of discipleship: following after the righteous from glory unto glory and from victory unto victory.

For this reason God gives double witness to His very great and precious promises: Word and deed. He gives us models to pattern ourselves after.

The Israelites had this two-fold witness when they went up to the Promised Land, but they failed to hear and heed. And thus they were defeated.

The lesson for us is clear: We must not imitate those faithless Jews at Kadesh. Instead, we must pattern ourselves after Abraham, Moses, Gideon, David, Daniel, and the disciples.

If we follow them, then their victory will become our victory.

We can thus face the odds . . . and win.

We can thus effect a changing of the guard.

CONCLUSION

"The Biblical concept of the covenant," according to Gary North, "is the Bible's most important doctrine relating to the relationship between God and man." This is because the covenant is the *pattern* for that relationship.

God's dealings with us are always covenantal. He judges us covenantally. He comforts us covenantally. He fellowships with us covenantally. He disciplines us, rewards us, and cares for us covenantally.

James B. Jordan describes the covenant as "the personal, binding, structural relationship among the Persons of God and His people. The covenant, thus, is a social structure." It is the divine-to-human/human-to-divine/human-to-human social structure. It is the means by which we approach, deal with, and know God and one another. It is the pattern of our relationship and our relationships.

According to Scripture, the covenant has at least five basic component parts. It begins with the establishment of God's nature and character: He is sovereign. Second, it proclaims God's authority over His people: He has established order and structure. Third, the covenant outlines His stipulations and ethics: the people have responsibility and responsibilities. Fourth, it establishes God's judicial see: He will evaluate and judge His people's work. And, finally, the covenant details God's very great and precious promises: the people have a future, an inheritance.

This outline of the covenant can be seen, in at least an oblique fashion, in God's dealings with Adam (Genesis 1:26-31; 2:16-25),

This has two immediate and very practical implications.

The first is legal. To acknowledge God's ordering structure is to acknowledge His subordinated authority in human institutions and situations. And to acknowledge His subordinated authority is to acknowledge the divine ordination and innate sacredness of such institutions and situations. In short, Christian political action is proper recognition and utilization of "the powers that be." We are to render unto Caesar the things that are Caesar's, all the while recognizing that Caesar is to be rendered unto God (see Chapter Two).

The second immediate and practical implication of God's ordering structure for political action is strategic. When we must pose an opposition to "the powers that be," that opposition must be honorable. In our political action, we must stand against the assaults of the enemies of God, but in so doing we must develop patterns of righteous resistance. If we do the right thing in the wrong way, we will not succeed. Nor will we glorify the name of Christ (see Chapter Seven).

Ethics

God has given us His Law. It is a guide for living and an expression of the unchanging standards of His rule. It is unchanging, eternal, trustworthy, and effectual.

Of course, the Law is not designed to effect salvation for men, but dominion. Salvation is a work of God's grace and no amount of Law-keeping can warrant that grace, it is a free gift. Even so, Law-keeping is not an optional affair for Christians. If the Great Commission is to be fulfilled, if the Dominion Mandate is to be satisfied, if godly cultural or political action is to be undertaken to any degree whatsoever, then God's ethical plumb line, as revealed in the Law, must be closely adhered to.

This has two immediate and very practical implications:

The first is legal. Since the idea of legalism—salvation by Law—is heretical, the humanistic and totalitarian fantasies of salvation by legislation and salvation by education must be stridently and stalwartly rejected by believers at all times and in all circumstances. Yet, we must not in the same breath commit an equal and opposite error: antinomian lawlessness. The Law is good in that it reveals the moral standards of God's rule, it convicts us of sin and leads us to Christ, it is a testimony to the nations, calling them to repentance, and, finally, it is a blueprint for living, a means for attaining our promised victory. Thus, as a provision of grace, the Law is to be utilized as the ethical standard for any and all Christian political action (see Chapter Three).

The second immediate and practical implication of God's established ethical decree for political action is strategic. We must not compromise. We must meet the challenge of politics with the same commitment to Biblical surety that we convey in every other sphere of life and Godliness. We must not waffle or waver when God's purposes are at issue. Of course, our steadfastness needs to be couched in humility and integrity, but never are we to sentimentally dull the edge of God's Word to man (see Chapter Eight).

Judgment

God judges sin. When a society refuses to acknowledge His sovereign rule, when it revolts against His ordering structure, when it spurns His ethical standards, it invites God's wrath. This is an inescapable principle: a nation reaps what it sows. If it sows obedience to God, it will reap blessings and abundance. But if it sows disobedience to God, it will reap judgment and paucity. God's sanctions are universal and immutable.

Christian political action recognizes the principle of judgment and works to protect the land from sin's consequences. It is the ultimate "strategic defense initiative."

This has two immediate and very practical implications:

The first is legal. The people of God are commissioned to be priests guarding the land. We are to protect society with our own righteousness—in word and in deed. Without that preserving and restraining juridical activity, our society is doomed. Without that seasoning and sanctifying mediatorial activity, our nation will perish. We must stand in the gap as Christ's ambassadors, thus integrating politics and faith (see Chapter Four).

The second immediate and practical implication of the reality of God's judgment for political action is strategic. We must pray. That may not sound like a particularly strategic political tactic, but in point of fact, prayer is the most powerful tool in the arsenal of political tactics God has given us. Prayer changes things. God hears and heeds our intercessions. When we are faithful to pray, God will move mountains, change hearts, and alter history. Thus, before we rally support, or call for conventions, or draft manifestos, or anything else, we must pray. That way, God receives all the glory, all the honor, and all the praise (see Chapter Nine).

Continuity

God has given us very great and precious promises. He has given us a tremendous inheritance.

Every Christian believes that at the time of the Second Advent Christ will visibly overcome the forces of Satan (Revelation 20:9). But what about now? What should the Church expect during the interim? What victory can the Bride of Christ expect to see? To put the question a bit more bluntly, are Christians joining the losing side in history when they join the Church? A lot of Christians think so. A lot of preachers preach so. But why? Does the Bible teach that the Church will lose in history? Absolutely not! We have the promise of victory. We have the promise of dominion. We have the promise of redemption. We have the promise of triumph, glory, and exaltation. Christian politics cannot survive in an atmosphere of pessimillenialism. In fact, the resurgence of Christian political action is evidence of a newly emerging evangelical post-pessimillenialism.

This has two immediate and very practical implications.

The first is legal. The task of the people of God in politics is to counter the effects of sin with the redemptive work of Christ. We are to take up our inheritance by reclaiming the land. Until now we've been so heavenly-minded that we've been no earthly good. But God wants us to be so heavenly-minded that we do the earth good. In short, we must take authority over the nations with the applied rule of Christ Jesus (see Chapter Five).

The second immediate and practical implication of our covenant inheritances for political action is strategic. God has set before us innumerable examples. Some good and some bad. Of course, we are to imitate the good and avoid the bad. This double witness should be the tactical pattern we utilize to face the odds going from glory unto glory and from victory unto victory. Only then will we be able to effect a *changing of the guard* (see Chapter Ten).

Part II
RECONSTRUCTION

This, of course, does not mean that Church and state are to have *nothing* to do with one another. On the contrary, God designed Church and state in such a way that they can cooperate with one another. They are to balance one another. They are to serve one another. They are to check one another. Though they are institutionally separate, their separation is not absolute and exclusive. There is no "wall of separation." Rather, Church and state are distinct but cooperative and interdependent. They are confederates.

Joseph Story, the foremost historian of the founding era, underscored this truth in his book, *Commentaries on the Constitution*, published in 1833. He wrote, ". . . the first Amendment was *not* intended to withdraw the Christian religion as a whole from the protection of Congress. . . . At the time, the general if not universal sentiment in America was, that Christianity ought to receive *encouragement* from the state so far as was compatible with the private rights of conscience and the freedom of worship. . . . Any attempt to level all religions, and to make it a matter of state policy to hold all in utter *indifference* would have created . . . universal *indignation*." The state was to cooperate with and encourage the Church.

At the same time, the Church was to cooperate with and encourage the state. It was the Church's job to teach the Bible, the common standard of Law for both Church and state. It was the Church's job to instruct believers in the basic principles of godly citizenship and righteous political action. It was the Church's job to mobilize the forces of mercy, truth, and justice in times of difficulty or crisis. It was the Church's job to recruit from the ranks of the congregation able men and women for service in the ministry of political action. It was the Church's job to expose evil and denounce sin, wherever it might be found, public and private, civil and congregational. It was the Church's job to encourage the magistrates, pray for them, support them, instruct them, and advise them.

The American system was thus set up as a *decentralized, confederated, and theocratic* social structure. It followed the Biblical order of *multiple jurisdictions, separate but cooperating,* under the *sovereignty of God and the rule of His Law.*

The current dogma of the "wall of separation" between Church and state is thus a far cry from our founding fathers' intent. It is, in fact, a *denial* of the multiplicity of institutions and jurisdictions. It cripples the Church and exalts the state. It denies the universal sovereignty of God over all institutions and asserts the absolute authority of the state. It excludes believers from their God-ordained ministry of social, cultural, and political involvement.

This "wall of separation" idea was slow to catch on in our nation. Until the War Between the States erupted, Christianity was universally encouraged *at* every level and *by* every level of the civil government. Then in 1861, under the influence of the radical Unitarians, the Northern Union ruled in the courts that the civil sphere should remain "indifferent" to the Church. After the war, that judgment was imposed on the Southern Confederation. One hundred years later in 1961, the erosion of the American system of Biblical checks and balances continued with the judicial declaration that all religious faiths were to be "leveled" by the state. By 1963 the courts were protecting and favoring a new religion — "humanism" had been declared a religion by the Supreme Court in 1940 — while persecuting and limiting Christianity. The government in Washington began to make laws "respecting an establishment of religion" and "prohibiting the free exercise thereof." It banned posting the Ten Commandments in school rooms, allowed the Bible to be read in tax supported institutions only as an historical document, forbade prayer in the public domain, censored seasonal displays at Christmas, Easter, and Thanksgiving, regulated Church schools and outreach missions, demanded IRS registration, and denied equal access to the media. It has stripped the Church of its jurisdiction and dismantled the institutional differentiation the founding fathers were so careful to construct.

In light of these historical realities and in light of the ten basic principles in the Biblical blueprint of political action, what should the Church do? What should the Church do to rectify the wrongs of a social and political system gone awry? What should

Let My people go, that they may hold a feast to Me in the wilderness (Exodus 5:1).

And again:

Let My people go, that they may serve Me in the wilderness
(Exodus 7:16).

As theologian David Chilton has written, "We know the story
of Israel. God forces Pharaoh to release them, and they went on to
inherit the Promised Land. But the really crucial aspect of the
whole Exodus event, as far as the *people's* activity was concerned,
was *worship*." And so it continues to be today. Chilton concludes,
"The orthodox Christian faith cannot be reduced to personal ex-
periences, academic discussions, or culture-building activity—as
important as all these are in varying degrees. The essence of Biblical religion is the worship of God. . . . True Christian reconstruction of culture is far from being simply a matter of passing Law X
and electing Congressman Y. Christianity is not a political cult. It
is the divinely ordained worship of the Most High God." (*Paradise
Restored*, Tyler, Texas: Reconstruction Press, 1985).

Notice what happens when God's people forget this very fundamental truth:

In the second year of King Darius, in the sixth month, on the
first day of the month, the word of the Lord came by Haggai the
prophet to Zerubbabel the son of Shealiel, governor of Judah, and
to Joshua the son of Jehozadak, the high priest, saying, "Thus
speaks the Lord of hosts, saying: 'This people says, "The time has
not come, the time that the Lord's house should be built." ' "

Then the word of the Lord came by Haggai the prophet, saying, "Is it time for you yourselves to dwell in your paneled houses,
and this temple to lie in ruins?" Now therefore, thus says the Lord
of hosts: "Consider your ways! You have sown much, and bring in
little; you eat, but do not have enough; you drink, but you are not
filled with drink; you clothe yourselves, but no one is warm; and
he who earns wages earns wages to put into a bag with holes."

"Thus says the Lord of hosts: 'Consider your ways! Go up to
the mountains and bring wood and build the temple, that I may

take pleasure in it and be glorified,' says the Lord. 'You looked for much, but indeed it came to little; and when you brought it home, I blew it away. Why?' says the Lord of hosts. 'Because of My house that is in ruins, while every one of you runs to his own house'" (Haggai 1:1-9).

When we neglect worship all else goes to seed.

Worship changes the shape of world history (Revelation 8:1-8; Matthew 6:19; John 20:23). Worship reorients us to God's plan, God's purpose, and God's program (Psalm 73:1-28). Worship brings about the demise of God's enemies and the exaltation of the righteous (Psalm 83:1-18).

This is why Paul is so insistent that our ministry of political action begin with *prayer* (1 Timothy 2:1-4). We are to pray benediction and blessing for those who honor God's Law in the civil sphere (Psalm 69:13-19), and we are to pray malediction and cursing for those who impugn God's Law in the civil sphere (Psalm 69:20-28). The practice of singing *Approbative Psalms* (Psalms of blessing, e.g.: 5, 7, 9, 20, 23, 25, 65, 75, 113) and *Imprecatory Psalms* (Psalms of cursing, e.g.: 2, 10, 35, 55, 59, 69, 79, 83, 94, 109, and 140) has long been the *first* recourse of political activism for the Church. And rightly so. If our *first* response is social or organizational or litigal or judicial, we are no better than the humanists, for we have put our trust in *human action* as the ultimate determiner of history.

We must begin to reassert the worshipping role of the Church in our day.

We must pray.

We must pray day and night, in season and out, in small groups and amidst the whole congregation, publicly and privately.

The Church must pray.

The Church must worship.

The Church must win.

Serving

God has called the Church to serve. And through service He grants us favor with the people. This is a fundamental principle of dominion in the Bible: *dominion through service.*

This principle is understood all too well by the humanists who run the modern Welfare State. They recognize that whatever agency serves the needs of the people will ultimately gain the allegiance of the people. So, they "serve." So, they continue the preposterous charade of government charity. And so, they gain dominion.

> And He said to them, "The kings of the Gentiles exercise lordship over them, and those who exercise authority over them are called 'benefactors.' But not so among you, let him be as the younger, and he who governs as he who serves. For who is greater, he who sits at the table, or he who serves? Is it not he who sits at the table? Yet I am among you as the One who serves. But you are those who have continued with Me in My trials. And I bestow upon you a kingdom, just as My Father bestowed one upon Me, that you may eat and drink at My table in My kingdom, and sit on thrones judging the twelve tribes of Israel" (Luke 22:25-30).

Sadly, Christians have not comprehended this link between charity and authority. They have not understood that dominion comes through service.

When people are needy, or fearful, or desperate, they seek out protection. They seek out benefactors. They seek out authorities with whom they can trade allegiance for security.

Early in our nation's history it was the Church that operated the hospitals, orphanages, alms houses, rescue missions, hostels, soup kitchens, welfare agencies, schools, and universities. The Church was a home to the homeless and a refuge to the rejected. As a result, the Church had authority. It earned its authority by serving.

Canvassing neighborhoods is fine. Registering voters is good. Evaluating candidates is important. Phone banks and direct mail centers and media campaigns are all necessary. *But,* if the Church *really* wants to make a *difference* in the political arena, it will become a sanctuary to the poor, the aged, the handicapped, the unborn, the abused, and the needy.

If you extend your soul to the hungry and satisfy the afflicted soul, then your light shall dawn in the darkness, and your darkness shall be as the noonday. The Lord will guide you continually, and satisfy your souls in drought, and strengthen your bones; you shall be like a watered garden, and like a spring of water, whose waters do not fail. Those from among you shall build the old waste places; you shall raise up the foundations of many generations; and you shall be called the Repairer of the Breach, the Restorer of Streets to Dwell In (Isaiah 58:10-12).

God will give us dominion. But only if the Church reasserts its serving role.

Prophesying

The Church must never be silent. Whenever and wherever sin exists, there the Church must be: exposing, rebuking, prophesying, teaching, and correcting.

Let no one deceive you with empty words, for because of these things the wrath of God comes upon the sons of disobedience. Therefore do not be partakers with them. For you were once darkness, but now you are light in the Lord. Walk as children of light (for the fruit of the Spirit is in all goodness, righteousness, and truth), proving what is acceptable to the Lord. And have no fellowship with the unfruitful works of darkness, but rather expose them (Ephesians 5:6-11).

When Planned Parenthood and the United States Department of Health and Human Services conspire together to *defraud* the American taxpayers of *Title XX allocations* in order to perpetuate the ghastly murder of unborn children, the Church must arise and *expose* them.

When the National Education Association and the United States Department of Education conspire together to steal away the minds and lives of our children, the Church must arise and *expose* them.

When the Internal Revenue Service and the Attorney General's office conspire together to require the registration and regulation of missions, ministries, and outreaches, the Church must arise and *expose* them.

When the National Organization for Women, the American Civil Liberties Union, the People for the American Way, the Trilateral Commission, the Abortion Rights Action League, and the American Atheist Society rattle their sabers against the people of God, the Church must arise and *expose* them. We must guard the gates of the city and sound the warnings.

> Son of Man, speak to the children of your people, and say to them: "When I bring the sword upon a land, and the people of the land take a man from their territory and make him their watchman, when he sees the sword coming upon the land, if he blows the trumpet and warns the people, then whoever hears the sound of the trumpet and does not take warning, if the sword comes and takes him away, his blood shall be on his own head. He heard the sound of the trumpet, but did not take warning; his blood shall be upon himself. But he who takes warning will save his life. But if the watchman sees the sword coming and does not blow the trumpet, and the people are not warned, and the sword comes and takes any person from among them, he is taken away in his iniquity; but his blood I will require at the watchman's hand" (Ezekiel 33:2-6).

If we refuse the prophetic mantle of John the Baptist (Matthew 14:3-12), of Elijah (1 Kings 21:1-25), and of Nathan (2 Samuel 12:1-13), in exposing the evil deeds of darkness in our day, the innocent and the helpless are sure to perish, and God's vast army will slumber through one Megiddo after another.

> Where there is no vision, the people perish (Proverbs 29:18, KJV).

> For if the trumpet makes an uncertain sound, who will prepare himself for battle? (1 Corinthians 14:8).

From its pulpits, in the media, through newsletters and pamphlets, with books and tracts, along the hedgeways, and over the grapevine the Church must arise and sound the prophetic alarm.

Judging

God established the Church as a *court*. He made it a *government*. Its jurisdictions, functions, and sanctions are different from the other governments God established, but they are no less real.

God invested the government of the family with the disciplinary power of the rod (Proverbs 13:24). If the family fails to exercise its government and its disciplinary power in a righteous manner, the whole society suffers (Proverbs 23:13-14).

God invested the government of the state with the disciplinary power of the sword (Romans 13:4). If the state fails to exercise its government and its disciplinary power in a righteous manner, the whole society suffers (Proverbs 31:1-9).

Likewise God has invested the Church with the disciplinary power of the *table* (1 Corinthians 11:17-34).

Up until this century, the Church's courts operated settling disputes between believers (1 Corinthians 6:1-11), meting out discipline on unrepentant members (1 Corinthians 5:1-13), and binding and loosing judgments against flagrant public sin (Matthew 18:15-20). At various times in history, Church courts so outshone civil courts in integrity that they came very nearly to the point of supplanting them.

> But he that is spiritual judgeth all things, yet he himself is judged of no man (1 Corinthians 2:15, KJV).

> Righteousness exalts a nation, but sin is a reproach to any people (Proverbs 14:34).

> A man will die for the lack of discipline, led astray by his own great folly (Proverbs 5:23).

> Do you not know that we shall judge angels? How much more, things that pertain to this life? (1 Corinthians 6:3).

Equipping

God has not only given the Church teaching, worshipping, serving, prophesying, and judging roles, He has given it an equipping role as well.

And He Himself gave some to be apostles, some prophets, some evangelists, and some pastors and teachers, for the equipping of the saints for the work of the ministry, for the edifying of the body of Christ, till we all come to the unity of the faith and the knowledge of the Son of God, to a perfect man, to the measure of the stature of the fullness of Christ (Ephesians 4:11-13).

The Church is to *train* God's people for the work of the ministry. If our nation is to have thoroughly equipped pastors, then the Church must train young men for the ministry of the Gospel (Romans 10:14-15). If our nation is to have thoroughly equipped teachers, then the Church must train young mothers and fathers for the ministry of education (Titus 2:1-15). If our nation is to have thoroughly equipped craftsmen, artists, musicians, philosophers, doctors, laborers, lawyers, scientists, and merchants, then the Church must train them for the ministry of acculturation (2 Timothy 3:16-17). And of course, if our nation is to have thoroughly equipped magistrates, then the Church must train them for the ministry of political action.

That does not mean that the Church must be the central depository for every discipline and specialty on the face of the earth —a *true* university. But it does mean that the Church must apply the Bible to every discipline and specialty on the face of the earth, *training* believers to exercise their various callings to the glory of God.

Now there are diversities of gifts, but the same Spirit. There are differences of ministries, but the same Lord. And there are diversities of activities, but it is the same God who works all in all. But the manifestation of the Spirit is given to each one for the profit of all (1 Corinthians 12:4-7, 12).

The Church should train young men and women for political action through information: distributing facts and figures on the central issues and candidates of the day, issuing educational literature, holding seminars, rallies, and workshops, etc.

The Church should train young men and women for political action through activism: picketing the death clinics of abortionists, demonstrating against the distribution of pornography, testifying at State Board of Education meetings, protesting IRS harassment of ministers and ministries, fighting for parental rights in the courts, etc.

If the Church doesn't train the next generation of magistrates, who will? The humanist establishment in the state schools? The humanist establishment in the major political parties? The humanist establishment in the media? The humanist establishment in the social service agencies? The humanist establishment in Washington, D.C.?

The Church must do the job of Eli and train up young Samuels (1 Samuel 2:11-3:21). The Church must do the job of Elijah and train up young Elishas (1 Kings 19:19-21). The Church must reassert its equipping role.

Action Agenda

What should the Church do? How should the Church apply the ten basic principles in the Biblical blueprint for political action?

First and foremost the Church must reassert its teaching, worshipping, serving, prophesying, judging, and equipping roles. The Church must be all that it was *meant* to be.

What this means in practical terms is that the Church must *really* go to work.

In *teaching*:

The Church should utilize the many resources God has given us to educate the people of God. The Church should teach classes on the Biblical principles of political action. The pulpit should become relevant to the issues. Pamphleteering should begin again in earnest. Candidate score cards should be distributed. Sunday schools, Bible studies, fellowship groups, missions organizations, and every other arm of the Church should be harnessed to inform and alert believers to the urgent crises of our day and their Biblical solutions.

In *worshipping*:

The Church should return to formal, organized, liturgically focused worship with specified prayer, sacramental integrity, cultural relevance, and spiritual efficacy. The Churches of our land should tap the enormous power of approbative and imprecatory psalmody. They should ring out with benedictory and maledictory fervor. They should address the issues, dilemmas, and crises the way the Church throughout the ages *always* has: in prayer, through worship.

In *serving:*

The Church should initiate programs of compassion and care. Biblical charity is *cheaper* than state welfare. Thus, it confronts the *tyranny of overbearing taxes.* Biblical charity is more *efficient* than state welfare. Thus, it confronts the *tyranny of overarching bureaucracy.* Biblical charity is *private.* Thus, it confronts the tyranny of power centralization. Biblical charity is *family-centered.* Thus, it confronts the tyranny of unaccountability. Biblical charity is *local.* Thus, it confronts the tyranny of statistical arbitrariness. Biblical charity is *temporary.* Thus, it confronts the tyranny of need—reinforcement and subsidization. When we care for the aged, the unborn, the neglected, and the poor we not only reclaim from the liberal humanists the moral high ground, we also reclaim from them the leverage of benevolence.

In *prophesying*:

The Church should speak out. The Church should call sin "sin." The Church should take a bold, uncompromising stand on the moral issues, identifying the enemies of the family, the enemies of life, the enemies of truth, the enemies of liberty, exposing them for what they are. We desperately need a Church that will willingly jeopardize its "reputation" in order to be counted with Noah, Moses, Elijah, Jeremiah, Amos, Ezekiel, and John the Baptist. We desperately need a Church that will willingly risk its IRS 501 (c) (3) designation for the sake of truth.

In *judging*:

The Church should once again hold court. The Church should take seriously its mandate from God to be a *real* government by binding and loosing, judging and discerning. The Church should begin to exercise discipline once again. It should reclaim its lost legacy of purity and integrity. It should reassert its role as the "Keeper of the Keys" (Matthew 16:19). It should balance the governments of state and family by being all it was meant to be.

In *equipping*:

The Church should take seriously its duty to train the next generation. It should take seriously its duty to be a light in the darkness, a well in the wilderness. The Church should make opportunities for its people to be involved in hands-on training in political action. It should identify the issues, pinpoint the principles, and mobilize the troops.

In *all these areas*:

The Church must *go to work*. The Church must reassert its roles. The Church must *do* everything within its power and jurisdiction to return this nation to a decentralized, confederated, and theocratic social structure.

And it must *do* it *now*.

Only then will we see a changing of the guard.

12

WHAT THE FAMILY SHOULD DO

Like the Church, the family has been entrusted with an institutional and governmental stewardship. God has established the family as a trustee over a specific jurisdiction.

The family's jurisdiction is *separate* from the Church's. And it is *separate* from the state's.

Family, Church, and state are each given unique tasks to accomplish. Consequently, they are not to meddle in each others' affairs.

They are to *cooperate*, however. They are to *coordinate* their efforts. Their checks and balances on one another enable society to be established on a decentralized, confederated, theocratic base.

Without the teaching and training of the Church, the state would be devoid of qualified leadership. But without the teaching and training of the family, the Church would be devoid of qualified leadership (1 Timothy 3:4-5, 12).

Of these three interrelated divine institutions, the family then is the most *basic* government. It is not the most *important*, mind you, just the most *basic*. The Church and the state *cannot* succeed if the family fails. The family is the *primary* agent of stability in a society.

The family is charged with the responsibility of infusing children with the principles of God's Law (Deuteronomy 6:6-7).

The family is charged with the responsibility of upbraiding, restraining, and rebuking unrighteous behavior (Proverbs 23:13-14).

134

The family is charged with the responsibility of balancing liberty with justice, freedom with responsibility, and licence with restriction (Deuteronomy 11:18-21).

The family is charged with the responsibility of being culture's *basic building* block (Genesis 9:1-7).

The family is central to virtually every societal endeavor under God: from education (Proverbs 22:6) to charity (1 Timothy 5:8), from economics (Deuteronomy 21:17) to spirituality (Ephesians 6:1-4), from the care of the aged (1 Timothy 5:3-13) to the subduing of the earth (Genesis 1:26-28).

And to all these responsibilities is added another. The family is central to the ministry of political action.

When the Family Fails

An interesting scenario is played out in the life of Samuel that Christians in our day had best pay heed to. It seems that the failure of his family life actually brought the entire nation of Israel to the brink of disaster.

> Now it came to pass when Samuel was old that he made his sons judges over Israel. The name of his firstborn was Joel, and the name of his second, Abijah; they were judges in Beersheba. But his sons did not walk in his ways; they turned aside after dishonest gain, took bribes, and perverted justice (1 Samuel 8:1-3).

Samuel was a *very* busy man. As the judge over Israel, he was forced to make the long and arduous "circuit from Bethel to Gilgal to Mizpah" (1 Samuel 7:16). His duties left little time for the diligent oversight of his home life in Ramah. He apparently attempted to rule his family from afar, but the result of that course, so sincerely undertaken, was nothing short of disastrous.

Samuel's neglect of family affairs was exposed in his sons after he had appointed them to be judges succeeding him. They failed to walk in a manner befitting righteousness. They turned aside after dishonest gain and accepted bribes and perverted justice. From their judicial seat in Beersheba, they exasperated the people and defiled judgement (1 Samuel 8:3).

This personal tragedy, as awful as it was for Samuel, was just
the beginning of his woes. The citizens of Israel, seeing the wickedness of Samuel's family and the senescence of Samuel himself,
began to panic. They began to fear for the future. They began to
fret over the stability of their cultural and political order.

> Then all the elders of Israel gathered together and came to
> Samuel at Ramah, and said to him, "Look, you are old, and your
> sons do not walk in your ways. Now make for us a king to judge us
> like all the nations" (1 Samuel 8:4-5).

The elders of the nation came together in Samuel's home to
confront the aged leader with their fears and to present him with
their demands. Samuel's family failure had undermined *national
security*. Thus, they wanted him to take *immediate* political action in
order to preserve life and liberty in the land. They wanted a king.
Like all the other nations around them, they wanted a king.

Samuel was grieved. His entire life's work had been comitted
to preserving the standard of Biblical Law and justice in Israel.
Now it seemed that his undersighted neglect at home was nullify-
ing his every accomplishment.

> But the thing displeased Samuel when they said, "Give us a
> king to judge us." So Samuel prayed to the Lord. And the Lord
> said to Samuel, "Heed the voice of the people in all that they say to
> you; for they have not rejected you, but they have rejected Me,
> that I should not reign over them. According to all the works which
> they have done since the day that I brought them up out of Egypt,
> even to this day—with which they have forsaken Me and served
> other gods—so they are doing to you also. Now therefore, heed
> their voice. However, you shall solemnly forewarn them, and show
> them the behavior of the king who will reign over them."
> So Samuel told all the words of the Lord to the people who asked
> him for a king. And he said, "This will be the behavior of the king
> who will reign over you: He will take your sons and appoint them
> for his own chariots and to be his horsemen, and some will run be-
> fore his chariots. He will appoint captains over his thousands and
> captains over his fifties, will set some to plow his ground and reap
> his harvest, and some to make his weapons of war and equipment

for his chariots. He will take your daughters to be perfumers, cooks, and bakers. And he will take a tenth of your grain and your vintage, and give it to his officers and servants. And he will take your menservants and your maidservants and your finest young men and your donkeys, and put them to his work. He will take a tenth of your sheep. And you will be his servants. And you will cry out in that day because of your king whom you have chosen for your-selves, and the Lord will not hear you in that day" (1 Samuel 8:6-18).

In desperation, Samuel attempted to warn the people of the inherent dangers of their scheme. There would be taxation. There would be conscription. There would be coercion. There would be tyranny. It was inevitable.

But the people could not be swayed.

Nevertheless the people refused to obey the voice of Samuel; and they said, "No, but we will have a king over us, that we also may be like all the nations, and that our king may judge us and go out before us and fight our battles" (1 Samuel 8:19-20).

The prospect of tyranny looked much better to the people than an eroding social and political order under Samuel's debauched family. A king and his tyranny then, it would be.

And Samuel heard all the words of the people, and he repeated them in the hearing of the Lord. So the Lord said to Samuel, "Heed their voice, and make them a king." And Samuel said to the men of Israel, "Every man go to his city" (1 Samuel 8:21-22).

Throughout his life, Samuel worked hard, traversing the countryside, weaving a social and political fabric impervious to the rending attacks of lawlessness, godlessness, and truthlessness. He poured himself into this work to the exclusion of all else — only to discover late in life that his sorely neglected family was unravel-ing every stitch.

When the family fails, the entire social and political system suffers. When the family fails, the Church suffers. When the family fails, the state suffers.

Thus, a key to rebuilding our nation through the ministry of political action relies to a great degree on the righteous participa-tion of families.

When the Family Succeeds

Just as Samuel's family failure had a dramatic and negative impact on the health of the entire nation, so Issachar's family success had a dramatic and positive impact on the health of the entire nation.

Issachar was the ninth son of Jacob, the fifth of Leah (Genesis 30:68; 35:23). The family descended from him consisted of four great tribal clans: the Tolaites, the Punites, the Joshubites, and the Shimranites (Numbers 26:23-24). At Sinai they numbered 54,000 (Numbers 1:29), but by the end of the desert wandering, when the people were counted at Kadesh Barnea, their population had swollen to 64,300 (Numbers 26:25).

Issachar's family was not merely huge. It was also a godly family.

> The sons of Issachar were *men*. They had *understanding* of the times, and *knew* what Israel ought to *do* (1 Chronicles 12:32).

The sons of Issachar included such heroes of the faith as Tola, the deliverer and judge (Judges 10:1-2), and Barak, the commander of Deborah's army (Judges 4:6-10; 5:1).

The sons of Issachar were among those named who rose up courageously against Sisera and Jabin (Judges 5:15), and who fought bravely beside David during the Ziklag exile (1 Chronicles 12:19-40).

So great was their valor, that the name of the sons of Issachar will forever be enshrined above one of the gates in the New Jerusalem (Ezekiel 48:33).

Such a wealth of godliness and faithfulness does not materialize in a family by chance. Family purity does not occur in a vacuum.

The sons of Issachar very obviously were nurtured in the admonition of the Lord (Ephesians 6:4). The sons of Issachar very obviously were raised up by godly parents who set the commandments of God upon their hearts, who talked about them when they sat at home, when they walked along the way, when they lay down, and when they rose up (Deuteronomy 6:6-7). The sons of

Issachar very obviously were taught, while still quite young, the way they should go—so, when they were old, they did not depart from it (Proverbs 22:6).

Notice the familiar refrain in the family lives of Moses (Exodus 2:1-10), Samson (Judges 13:2-25), David (Ruth 4:13-22), John the Baptist (Luke 1:5-25), Paul (Philippians 3:4-8), and Timothy (2 Timothy 3:14-15). Like these other godly men of valor, the sons of Issachar knew the joys of righteous homes. And the nation was enhanced immeasurably by it.

The sons of Issachar "understood the times." They "knew what Israel should do." And they did it. As a family.

What can the family do to restore our nation's godly foundations? How can it contribute to the ministry of political action?

It can create a righteous home atmosphere.

It can inculcate holiness.

It can build sturdy foundations of discipline, nurture, and love.

It can saturate its progeny with the Word of Truth and Life.

In short, it can put all the raging issues of our day into perspective.

Putting Issues in Perspective

Thankfully, the long and protracted feud between Christian families and social action is now all but over.

Unfortunately, the cease-fire was predicated on something other than full Biblical authority.

Over the last several years, our families have awakened from a carefully sequestered cultural sleep . . . in horror. We saw the awful consequences of pagan humanism in unchecked promiscuity, runaway materialism, no-fault easy divorce, and abortion on demand. We saw the need to do something more than simply snatch brands from the flickering flames of hell. We saw the need for action.

As commendable as this action has been, it was and is established upon woefully weak premises. As necessary as the action has been, it was and is established upon pitifully inadequate theology.

Most Christian families fight abortion on the basis of "a right
to life." We fight injustice on the basis of "a right to freedom." And
we fight poverty on the basis of "a right to food." In short, we have
established our movement on human rights.

The Bible does not guarantee human rights. At the time of the
fall, man lost all rights except the right to death (Romans 5:12).
"The wages of sin is death," says Paul (Romans 6:23), and "All
men have sinned" (Romans 3:23). Thus, every second of life on
earth is the undeserved gift of God. Restraint of sin is found in
God's Law, not in some subjective theory of abstract rights.

What this means is that all protection, all justice, all compassion, and all fairness are given to men on the basis of grace and an
adherence to the Word of God, not rights. The Bible does not
teach human rights as such: privilege apart from responsibility. It
teaches human blessing and protection stemming from grace-
provoked obedience.

As godly families we must fight for the oppressed, for the unborn, for the hungry, for the poor, and for the dispossessed, but
not because of their rights. We must fight for them, not on the
basis of a human assertion of what is good and fair. We must fight
for life and liberty on the basis of the only absolute, the only
standard, the only immutable mandate that exists: the Word of
God. If we attempt to protect the unborn and the dispossessed
with rights, we will inevitably fail, for we have asserted no higher
value than that of the gay rights movement, the women's rights
movement, or the abortion rights movement. But if we attempt to
protect the unborn and the dispossessed with an uncompromised
and unapologetic stand on the Word of God, we will inevitably
succeed. Justice is attained only when the Law of God is obeyed.

We cannot hope to win the battle for life if we continue to use
the same tactics as the humanists. All of their gains have come as
they have asserted the primacy of rights. Let's not make the same
mistake. Instead of standing up for rights, it is time to stand up
for the Bible. Instead of claiming judicial immunity, it is time to
demonstrate to a fallen and corrupt culture that the only hope for
justice, mercy, order, and life is in the strict obedience to the Word

of God. The only guarantee of life for the unborn will come, not as we uphold the right to life, but as we uphold the Word of Life.

Only the family can bring this perspective to the ministry of political action, because it is the family that is charged with the task of education (Deuteronomy 6:1-9). Raising our children in the nurture and admonition of the Lord (Ephesians 6:4) is the *most subversive* moral and political action a family can take against the rights-oriented liberal humanist establishment.

Educating the Next Generation

"A nation at risk." That's how the United States Department of Education describes the state of the Union, as viewed from the classroom.

Public education in the United States is a dismal failure. Johnny can't read and Susie can't spell. Willie can't write and Alice can't add. Teacher competency is down. Administrative effectiveness is down. Everything to do with government approved, government controlled, government designed schools is down . . . everything, that is, except crime, drug abuse, illicit sex, and the cost to taxpayers.

According to the U.S. Department of Education, 23 million Americans are functionally illiterate. Just fifty years ago, only 1.5% of white, native-born Americans struggled with illiteracy. Today that figure has peaked at nearly 10%. Urban blacks fifty years ago faced an illiteracy rate of about 9%. Today the figure is an astonishing 40%. And this, despite a multi-billion dollar splurge by the government schools and their humanistic cohorts in the National Education Association (NEA).

The icing on the cake of ill report is that the NEA and the schools are not content to despoil the millions of children under their superintendence in the public school districts. They want to rape and pillage the rest of the land as well by pulling private schools, alternative schools, and Christian schools down to their level of impotence and incompetence. They know that when Christian parents take their God-given responsibility seriously, their whole debauched house of cards is jeopardized. And their plan to despoil our land with their perversity is threatened with utter failure. So, they want to shut the door of opportunity, the door of freedom of choice for the state's school children. They want to outlaw anything and everything but the schools they control.

But they want to do it all in the name of the public good, you understand. One NEA board member recently suggested that Christian schools and home schools were a *menace* to the health and welfare of children, unable as they are to provide an appropriate physical education program.

That's like the pot calling the kettle black. A recent survey of America's public schools found the lowest level of physical fitness performance in over a decade. The President's Council on Physical Fitness found that 40% of boys aged 6-12 and 70% of all the girls could not do more than one pull up. 55% of the girls could not do any. Half of the girls aged 6-17 and 30% of the boys aged 6-12 could not run a mile in less than 10 minutes. 45% of the boys and 55% of the girls could not hold their chin over a raised bar for more than 10 seconds. 40% of the boys could not even reach beyond their toes while seated on a floor with legs outstretched.

So much for the humanists arguments! Not only have the public schools failed to raise the level of students' brains above pudgy mush, but they have failed to do it with their bodies as well.

And they want to shut down any and all alternatives to their ineffective and unproductive system?

We are indeed "a nation at risk."

Unless, of course, Christian families go to work and fight the political fight necessary to preserve liberty in the land.

Besides keeping our children in private Christian schools or home schools, Christian parents must begin to attend our State Board of Education's public hearings. We must keep in touch with our local school board.

Go to the PTA meetings. Review the various budgets. Testify at the hearings. Stand in the gap. Fight the fight. Just because our kids don't go to public schools doesn't mean that we should ignore what they are doing with billions upon billions of our tax dollars. If we don't stand up for our interests and the interests of our

Christian-schooled or home-schooled children, no one will.

Whenever the state raises the issues of zoning restrictions, or curriculum regulations, or testing prerequisites, or board superintendence, Christian families must take up the banner of political action. We must lobby. We must legislate. We must litigate. We must win.

The future depends on it.

Our children depend on it.

Dollars and Sense

But in order to win, we'll need more than zeal.

One of the most basic realities of modern civic life is the high cost of political action. Politics is expensive.

It is not enough to master the issues, demonstrate integrity, and forge alliances any longer. To succeed in politics these days, candidates and coalitions need money. And lots of it.

Modern campaigns spend most of their time and most of their energy raising money. They turn to corporations, to labor unions, to political action committees (PACs), and to banks in a desperate drive to out-razzle, out-dazzle, and out-spend the opposition.

You would think that amidst all that high-powered hype and hustle the "lowly" family would be of little or no significance. But that is just not so.

God has ordained the family to be the primary agent of the economy within society (Deuteronomy 21:17). Not the corporation. Not the conglomerate. Not the multinational megalith. But the family.

With a bare minimum of entrepreneurial effort, a grassroots coalition of Christian families could literally raise millions of dollars for godly candidates and causes. It *can* be done.

In the state of Texas for example, God has raised up men like David Davidson and Adrian Van Zelfdon who have begun to work with grassroots family fund raising with great success. (For more information about their programs and how you can adapt them to your own state, write to: Coalition of Politically Active Christians [COPAC], Post Office Box 163681, Austin, Texas,

78716; and The Texas Grassroots Coalition, 95001 Capitol of Texas North, #304, Austin, Texas, 78759).

If we are to be protected against the ravages of modern humanism by reclaiming modern politics, then our families must enter the fray with *both* dollars *and* sense.

Action Agenda

What should families do in light of the ten basic principles in the Biblical blueprint for political action? What should families do to effect the changing of the guard?

In *nurturing*:

Families should nurture righteousness in their midst. They should disciple their children, involve them in a good Bible believing church, and build a multigenerational testimony of truth and valor.

In *educating*:

Families should build for the future. We cannot expect to perpetuate a godly line if we offer our children up to Molech by sacrificing them in the temple of the public schools. We must take responsibility for our children's education. We must either school them ourselves at home or we must find a good parent-directed private Christian school and pay the price for the future.

In *protecting*:

It is not enough, though, simply to try to create a secure ecology at home in which to nurture and educate our children. Families must take action against the forces of unrighteousness in the educational system, the abortion industry, the pornography network, and the child abuse industry. And that takes dollars. Lots of them. But being the primary agent of economy, the family is the best institution to raise those dollars and channel those dollars into the right hands.

Families today must, like the sons of Issachar of yore, have an understanding of the times, and know what ought to be done.

And then we must do it (James 1:22).

Otherwise our families will go the way of Samuel's, and our nation will go the way of Israel's. And that would not be a pretty sight.

13

WHAT YOU SHOULD DO

One church can make a real difference.

One family can make a real difference.

Even one person can make a real difference.

Every vote matters.

In 1645, Oliver Cromwell gained control of England by *one vote*. In 1776, *one vote* determined that English, not German, would be the official American language. In 1845, *one vote* brought Texas into the Union. In 1860, *one vote* determined that the radical Unitarians would gain control of the Republican party, thus sparking the War Between the States. In 1923, *one vote* gave Adolf Hitler control of the Nazi party. In 1960, John F. Kennedy defeated Richard Nixon for the presidency by less than *one vote* per precinct. George McGovern and Paul Laxalt first won their seats in the U.S. Senate by less than *one vote* per precinct, while Jeremiah Denton and Paula Hawkins lost theirs by less than *one vote* per precinct. The drubbing Republican candidates received in the mid-term elections of 1986 averaged out to less than *one vote* lost per precinct nationwide.

Every vote matters.

The fact is, never once in the history of our Republic has a majority of the citizens elected a president. Just 26.7% of the electorate put Ronald Reagan in the White House in the "landslide" of 1980. In 1836, less than 12% made Martin Van Buren the chief executive.

Since only about 60% of the people are registered to vote and only about 35% of those actually bother to go to the polls, a can-

satisfactory. But strive to get 100%, even if you need to do a little follow-up work after all is said and done. After all, *every vote matters*.

Getting the Word Out

Some Christians are hesitant to get involved in the political process simply because they are uncertain about issues or candidates. Politics is so complex. The campaigns are filled with accusations and counter-accusations, contradictions and counter-contradictions. How can anyone know for certain what the truth is?

We certainly can't depend on the newspapers, radio, or television to give us the straight story. Information from the media is all too often gathered by questionable people from questionable sources who work for questionable organizations. The media specializes in name recognition, and they are able to create a desired image by controlling (or sometimes withholding) information. The result of voting under this counsel is that responsible Christians may be influenced by name recognition and an "honest" image in the press only to see later that these men stand for principles totally opposed to God's Word.

Thus, *you* will need to be sure to have plenty of well-researched, non-partisan literature on hand. If there are no "Christian scorecards" available in your area, do your *own* homework. Call or go by the various campaign offices and ask where each candidate stands on such issues as abortion, pornography, taxes, and commercial regulation. If a candidate is an incumbent, obtain a copy of his voting record. Tally the results of your findings and then make copies for distribution at church or in your community.

Of course, if you want to get a bit more ambitious than simply holding a coffee clatch after church handing out your literature, you may want to tap into the direct mail boom.

Utilizing the mails, a small name list, and a personal computer, you can make a *real* difference. You can *really* get the word out and ultimately you get the vote out.

The master of political mailing lists is Richard Viguerie, a member of the "new right" who began with a list of donors to

Barry Goldwater's ill-fated presidential campaign in 1964. Viguerie was able to recognize something early on: Goldwater had generated more small donations than any presidential candidate in modern times. There were a lot of "true believers" out there on the grass roots level. He was wise enough to gain access to those early "new right" grass roots lists.

With those lists he was able to make a technological end run for conservative and Christian causes. The fruit of nearly two decades of labor became evident in 1980 when Viguerie's "new right" lists helped usher in "The Reagan Revolution."

There are limits to Viguerie's lists, however. The biggest problem is their size. Because over the years he has collected so many names, small campaigns really cannot afford to use his services.

So two of Viguerie's former employees, Larry Pratt, a Washington lobbyist and a former member of the Virginia State Assembly, and computer whiz Frank Slinkman spent two years designing and redesigning a mailing list program to meet the needs of local candidates. They designed the program for the TRS-80 Model I, but they soon upgraded it for the Model III, and the IBM. The program is called POLSYS.

Each POLSYS floppy disk can store more than 1,000 names, and under each name there are a staggering number of "user-defined variables." Among these are two telephone numbers, spouse's first name, precinct (four-digit variable), 38 individualized codes, eight "yes-no" variables, and contribution data such as amount, date, and source.

Now just consider for a moment what this little program provides Christians in the mainstream of political action. You can identify supporters instantly or scan the list for everyone who has given more than $50 since a certain date. The contribution file can absorb any number of entries, so you can contact people who have contributed to your campaigns five times, made five $15 contributions, or whatever.

The 38 individualized codes might identify the person on the list as a media representative, newsletter writer, Kiwanis member, Baptist, Presbyterian, Lions Club member and so forth. The survey data might include pro-abortion or anti-abortion, pro-gun control or anti-gun control, pro-ERA or anti-ERA, pro-defense spending or anti-defense spending.

So, for example, a Christian in politics could tell his personal computer to pull out the names of everyone who is pro-life, pro-family, and has given at least three times in the past and has attended at least one meeting where he spoke. The computer scans the files in less than three seconds and produces the names of everyone who fits this description.

POLSYS designer, Larry Pratt tells the following tale with relish. "When I was in the Virginia Legislature, the State Board of Health was committed to putting in a regulation that would have used public funds to finance abortions. We figured that the vote would be 7 to 2 or 8 to 1 in favor.

"We think the Board tipped off the pro-abortion forces in May 1980 that there would be public hearings in September. The opposition had almost five months to organize. I was a state assemblyman, and I didn't hear about the hearings until mid-August. But I had POLSYS, and they didn't."

Pratt went down to his basement, went through his data base of 9,000 names, and pulled out 7,500 pro-life people. The printer cranked out the labels, and that evening he mailed a letter asking the life advocates to write to the Board of Health, both as a group and as individual members. He gave the date of the hearings.

The result? Within two weeks, the Board received 9,000 letters, petitions, and telegrams. In five months the pro-abortion forces, using traditional methods, had mustered only 2,000. In addition, more than 500 pro-lifers showed up at the hearings.

"It was incredible," Pratt says. "My letter didn't mention the Governor, but his desk was flooded with protests. He said later that in two terms, this was one of the three top responses—'spontaneous outpourings,' he called them—he had received. Well, maybe the other two were spontaneous. Ours *looked* spontaneous, and, in one sense, it really was. I hadn't told people to write to him. But POLSYS made it look spontaneous. The opposition never knew what hit them."

The Board voted in favor of the regulation, 5 to 4. The Governor vetoed it. One man, with $6,000 in equipment plus postage, had engineered the whole event, and the letter raised $3,000 in contributions for pro-life forces.

This is the politics of the future, whichever side of the political spectrum candidates may be on. The candidate who fails to perceive this now is unlikely to survive the 1980s. Christians called to the ministry of political action must realize this.

We must get the word out. One way or another.

Turning Out the Vote

As important as registration and information distribution are, all our efforts count for nothing if we can not turn our people out to the polls on election day.

Put your registration volunteers on a telephone committee, dividing up the church roll, calling everyone to remind him of the vote.

When making a call, the volunteer should:

First, identify himself as a member of the church.

Second, remind the person called that Christians have a duty to vote. If the pastor has made any statement urging the church people to vote, quote the pastor.

Third, inform the voter of:

The place and address of the poll for his precinct.

The date and time the poll will be open.

And the availability of transportation if needed.

Fourth, ask the voter to remind the other members of his family to vote.

Be sure to be brief and don't extend the conversation, but do ask directly for commitment to go to the polls on election day.

If only half of the 33 million people in the United States who claim to be "born again" would actually make it to the polls and vote with an informed conscience, we could turn our nation around. Christians would become the most important swing vote in modern political history.

The Pen Is Mightier Than the Sword

Once an election is over, the battle has only just begun.

The pen is mightier than the sword. Or, so they say. And even a cursory glance at the vast annals of history seems to bear that out, not merely as truism, but as the truth.

What do Plato and Marx, Thucidides and Newton, Calvin and Darwin, Locke and Hobbes, Luther and Rousseau, Augustine and Hegel all have in common? They all shook up the world, changed the world with a mere stroke of the pen . . . some for great good, some for great evil. Instead of wielding sword and spear, they parried and reposted on the printed page. Instead of commanding cavalries and leading assaults, *they wrote*. They wrote books and pamphlets. They wrote articles and tracts. They wrote letters and manifestos. They gripped the world and marshalled legions not with saber rattling, but with words. Words and ideas.

And what words! Words to topple kings and queens and presidents. Words to spark revolutions. Words to transform cultures.

At a time when Christians in America are calling for massive changes in the moral ecology of the land, in the ideological foundations of the culture, it is odd to note our obvious in-attention and ill-attention to words. Only one out of every ten Christians has ever written his representative in Congress. Only one out of every twenty has ever written a letter to the editor of his local newspaper. Only one out of every 700 has ever written an article or tract or pamphlet. This, despite the fact that the issues at hand are life and death issues. This, despite the fact that assaults against liberty, justice, and truth have grown to crisis proportions. This, despite the fact that one or two well-written, well-timed letters can turn the tide, wielding tremendous influence.

Perhaps it's time for Christians to drown the enemies of the Gospel — in a sea of ink. Perhaps it's time for Christians to bombard them — with words. Perhaps it's time to prove once again that indeed the pen *is* mightier than the sword.

Make a difference.

Write your State Senators and Representatives. Contact your

district's member of the School Board. Drop a note to the Attorney General, the Speaker of the House, the Governor, and the Lieutenant Governor. Correspond with your magistrates in Washington.

But, be sure to utilize these contacts for the greatest positive effect.

So for instance, take great care in the composition and structure of your letter. In congressional offices, your opinions will usually receive consideration proportionate to the *personal* attention you seem to have given them. Pre-printed postcards and form letters, even petitions, simply don't receive much attention. A personal, neat, well-thought-out letter shows your magistrate (or his staff) that you *really care* about the issue.

Also, be precise and concise. Your letter should *briefly* outline how and why a particular bill or proposal or issue will adversely affect you, your family, your church, your job, and/or your community. If you really feel that you *must* write a long, detailed letter, be sure to consolidate most of your concerns in the first paragraph or so—that may be all that will be read.

Obviously, your letter should be polite and respectful, but don't softpedal the issues. Identify your concerns tactfully but straightforwardly, and then request *specific* action. Be encouraging, not abrasive. Like most of us, magistrates and their staffs are likely to be polarized all the more by a demanding or threatening letter.

While you're at it, it would be wise to ask the magistrate to respond in one way or another to your concerns. And if he votes favorably on this or another key issue, be sure to respond yourself. Write back thanking him for his responsible and godly representation of the community's interests.

As a final checklist: First, make certain that your letter is signed and dated with your name, address, and phone number clearly noted. Second, make sure it is timely (a magistrate is not responsible to consider your views if he doesn't hear from you until *after* a critical vote). And third, make sure it is neat, grammatically correct, and conceptually focused—if your magistrate can't really figure out what you're talking about, your letter hasn't done a whole lot of good.

The same basic rules apply to letters to the editor or op-ed pieces. Whatever you do, make your views heard. And make your words count.

Working Within the System

The American political system was designed by our founding fathers to be a decentralized, confederated, and theocratic republic. That means it was designed to operate from the *bottom up*. The policies, procedures, and platforms of both major parties begin at the precinct level.

Fewer than 3% of all voters ever even attend a precinct convention or caucus. In most precincts, that means that all you have to do is *show up* and you can shape national policy! A core group of between five and ten individuals can almost always *control* a precinct meeting. And it is the precinct meeting that elects delegates, sends resolutions, and formulates platforms for the district, state, and national party conventions.

Go to your precinct convention *prepared*. Have your resolutions typed and printed in triplicate.

Get neighbors, friends, and church members in your precinct together for a pre-caucus strategy session. Decide on a convention chairman and an agenda that you all can vote for en masse. Then go expecting to *win*.

Propose and push through resolutions calling for an immediate end to abortion, pornography, entrepreneurial regulation, higher taxes, and all the other liberal humanist boondoggles of our day. Work for a pro-life, pro-family, pro-business platform by having *specific* recommendations to make.

But don't make your political activism a one night stand, or you will lose all credibility. Get involved in the party network. Volunteer to work in the campaign headquarters. Work the phone banks. Take a turn as a poll watcher. Go to the city Council meetings. Join the PTA. Get involved. Remember: dominion comes through service.

Working Outside the System

In a political ecology controlled to the uttermost by the enemies of God, there may be times when the system seems only to work against the cause of Christ.

Church historians for years have pondered with inquisitive awe the uncharacteristically ferocious persecution that the New Testament era believers faced. In a day of tolerance, prosperity, and governmental stability, why did the intense public outrage break forth? Was there something about the early Church rituals that particularly irked the Romans?

Almost unquestionably not. The Empire sheltered within its folds all manner of esoterica and erratica. In comparison, the Church was tame to say the least.

Was there something about the early Church doctrine that particularly irked the Romans?

Again, that's highly unlikely. Mystery cults, occultic covens, and theosophic sects of the wildest order thrived under the tolerant wings of the Empire.

So what was it that singled Christianity out to be so awfully *despised* by the civil magistrates and the populace at large?

According to Francis Schaeffer, "The early Christians died because they would not obey the State in a *civil* matter . . . they were *civil rebels*. The Roman State did not care what anybody believed religiously; you could believe anything or you could be an atheist. But you had to pay homage to Caesar as a sign of your loyalty to the State." (*A Christian Manifesto*, Westchester, IL: Crossway Books, 1981).

The Christians said "no." That is why they were thrown to the lions. They were civil rebels. They were not imprisoned, beaten, reviled, stoned, exiled, and executed because of their peculiar dogmas. They met with persecution because they refused to obey the government.

An excerpt from the *Law of the Twelve Tables* stated that no Roman citizen was to "have gods on his own, neither new ones nor strange ones, but only those instituted by the State." Another statute in the *Celsus Tables* aimed specifically at the Christians stated that "they form among themselves secret societies that exist *outside* the *system of laws* . . . an obscure and mysterious community founded on *revolt* and on the advantage that accrues from it." And, according to the great second century Christian defense attorney Athenagoras, prosecution proceeded on two points: "That we do not sacrifice and that we do not believe in the same gods as the state."

The historian, Dio Cassius, confirmed this emphasis in Roman law during the reign of Domitian. He stated that the Emperor "had executed, among many others, the consul Flavius Clemens, even though he was a cousin of his, and his wife, Flavia Domitilla, who was also related to Domitian. The accusation against both was that of *treason*. On the basis of this accusation, many others who had adopted the customs of the Jewish Christians were also condemned. Others were at the very least, deprived of their property or suffered banishment."

Clearly, the Roman government saw the Christians not simply as an arcane religious group, but as a *band of civil insurrectionists*. They were undermining the *authority of the state* by *claiming a higher allegiance*. Christianity knocked the state from its messianic pedestal, thus it was *anarchy* in the eyes of the imperial protectors.

Any time the state attempts to make itself "the center of all human loyalties, the goal of all human aspirations, the source of all human values, and the final arbiter of all human destiny," says John W. Whitehead, "conflict becomes inevitable" (*The Second American Revolution*, David C. Cook, 1982).

Such was the case in Rome.

And, amazingly, such is the case in our own day.

Why was there such severe persecution against Christians in the days of Imperial Rome? For the same reasons that Christians are being harassed today so brutishly by pro-abortionists, People for the American Way, the NOW, the IRS, the state Boards of Education, and the ACLU: the Law of God is higher than the law of men. And in the monolithic modern federalism, the law of men unavoidably contravenes the precepts of Scripture. Christians, thus, are branded as subversives to the welfare of the society.

If so — so be it!

Peter, James, and John had to work outside the system for a time in order to get the message of the Gospel out (Acts 4:19-20). Ultimately the Gospel won and the Roman Empire was converted. But until that had occurred the disciples of Christ had to find other means to effect the ministry of political action.

At the present time the laws of many states and municipalities hinder Christians from fulfilling our God-ordained responsibilities: *rescuing* the perishing (Proverbs 24:10-12), *educating* our children in the Law of God (Deuteronomy 6:1-9), and *caring* for the poor and homeless (Isaiah 58:6-12). What are we to do when such civil tyranny actually *excludes* us from the system. Do we have to resort immediately to civil disobedience?

Not at all.

In the Scriptures, God's people at various times and in various situations demonstrate a number of different reactions to civil tyranny that involve working outside the system. When the state oversteps its bounds and begins to violate God's immutable law, believers have several models of tactical action from which to choose.

For instance, Daniel, when asked to violate Scripture, simply utilized the tactic of the wise appeal. Instead of instantly indulging belligerent rebellion against divinely instituted authority, he proposed an alternative course of action, which ultimately gained for him the favor of the court (Daniel 1:8-16).

Similarly, the Apostle Paul, when faced with an ungodly and unscrupulous jury, exercised the tactic of lawyer delay. Instead of reviling the authorities, instead of outright rebellion, instead of sullen submission, Paul upheld the integrity of God's law through the appellate process (Acts 25:1-27).

Moses, when faced with the awful oppression of God's people, began a very forthright lobbying initiative. Rather than advocating an armed rebellion, he sought a change in Pharaoh's tyrannical policy. His whole approach, though from without, was to force the evil system of Egypt to change from within (Exodus 5:1-21).

Obadiah was the chief counsel to King Ahab, perhaps the

your money in the future by giving to godly candidates. Attend rallies. Work at the polls. Just get involved.

Initiating *activism*:

You should make your faith visible. Let your testimony be clear to all. Write letters. Make resolutions. Compile a mailing list. Spend some time in the picket lines at a local abortion clinic. Participate in a home schoolers' rally. Support a local baby rescue. Use alternative resistance tactics.

Whatever you do, do all for the glory of God, under the authority of the Word.

Whatever you do, do all in light of the ten basic principles of the Biblical blueprint for political action.

Whatever you do, *do it now*. Only then will we witness a changing of the guard.

FOR FURTHER READING

Bring the cloak that I left with Carpus at Troas when you come—and the books, especially the parchments (2 Timothy 4:13).

Walter Brueggemann, *The Land* (London: SPCK, 1978).

Lynn Buzzard and Paula Campbell, *Holy Disobedience: When Christians Must Resist the State* (Ann Arbor, Michigan: Servant Books, 1984).

David Chilton, *Paradise Restored: An Eschatology of Dominion* (Tyler, Texas: Institute for Christian Economics, 1985).

_____. *Productive Christians in an Age of Guilt-Manipulators*, 3rd rev. ed. (Tyler, Texas: Institute for Christian Economics, 1985).

Gary DeMar, *God and Government: A Biblical and Historical Study* (Atlanta, Georgia: American Vision Press, 1982).

_____. *God and Government: Issues in Biblical Perspective* (Atlanta, Georgia: American Vision Press, 1984).

_____. *God and Government: The Restoration of the Republic* (Atlanta, Georgia: American Vision Press, 1986).

_____. *Ruler of the Nations: The Biblical Blueprint for Civil Government* (Fort Worth, Texas: Dominion Press, 1987).

George Grant, *Bringing in the Sheaves: Transforming Poverty into Productivity* (Atlanta, Georgia: American Vision Press, 1985).

_____. *The Dispossessed: Homelessness in America* (Westchester, Illinois: Crossway Books, 1986).

_____. *In the Shadow of Plenty: Biblical Principles of Welfare and Poverty* (Fort Worth, Texas: Dominion Press, 1986).

_____. *LifeLight: The Bible and the Sanctity of Human Life* (Ft. Worth, Texas: Dominion Press, 1987).

James B. Jordan, *Entangling Alliances: Christianity and International Relations* (Fort Worth, Texas: Dominion Press, 1987).

_____. *Judges: God's War Against Humanism* (Tyler, Texas: Geneva Ministries, 1985).

_____. *The Law of the Covenant: An Exposition of Exodus 21-23* (Tyler, Texas: Institute for Christian Economics, 1984).

Vishal Mangalwadi, *Truth and Social Reform* (New Delhi, India: Nivedit Books, 1986).

Gary North, *Inherit the Earth* (Fort Worth, Texas: Dominion Press, 1987).

_____. *Liberating Planet Earth* (Fort Worth, TX: Dominion Press, 1987).

_____. *Moses and Pharaoh: Dominion Religion Versus Power Religion* (Tyler, Texas: Institute for Christian Economics, 1985).

_____. *Unconditional Surrender* (Tyler, Texas: Geneva Divinity School Press, 1982).

_____. *The Sinai Strategy: Economics and the Ten Commandments* (Tyler, Texas: Institute for Christian Economics, 1986).

Dennis Peacocke, *Christ the Liberator of the Nations* (Tustin, California: Metz Communications, 1987).

Mary Pride, *The Big Book of Home Learning* (Westchester, Illinois: Crossway Books, 1986).

_____. *The Child Abuse Industry* (Westchester, Illinois: Crossway Books, 1986).

Rushdoony, R. J., *The Institutes of Biblical Law* (Nutley, New Jersey: Craig Press, 1973).

_____. *The Nature of the American System* (Tyler, Texas: Thoburn Press, 1978).

_____. *Politics of Guilt and Pity* (Tyler, Texas: Thoburn Press, 1978).

_____. *This Independent Republic* (Tyler, Texas: Thoburn Press, 1978).

Schaeffer, Francis, *A Christian Manifesto* (Westchester, Illinois: Crossway Books, 1981).

Phyllis Schlafly ed., *Child Abuse in the Classroom* (Westchester, Illinois: Crossway Books, 1984).

Ray Sutton, *That You May Prosper: Dominion By Covenant* (Fort Worth, Texas: Dominion Press, 1987).

_____. *Who Owns the Family?* (Fort Worth, Texas: Dominion Press, 1986).

Robert Thoburn, *The Christian and Politics* (Tyler, Texas: Thoburn Press, 1984).

Henry Van Til, *The Calvinistic Concept of Culture* (Philadelphia: Presbyterian and Reformed, 1959).

Peter Waldron with George Grant, *Rebuilding the Walls: A Biblical Strategy for Restoring America's Greatness* (Brentwood, Tennessee: Wolgemuth and Hyatt Publishers, 1987).

E. C. Wines, *The Hebrew Republic* (Uxbridge, Massachusetts: American Presbyterian Press, 1980).

RESOURCES FOR ACTION

Put on the whole armor of God, that you may be able to stand against the wiles of the devil (Ephesians 6:11).

Book Services

American Vision, P.O. Box 720515, Atlanta, Georgia, 30328.

Dominion Book Service, P.O. Box 8204, Fort Worth, Texas, 76124.

Fairfax Christian Books, P.O. Box 6941, Tyler, Texas, 75711.

Government Printing Office, Washington, D.C., 20402.

Puritan and Reformed Discount Books, 1319 Newport Gap Pike, Wilmington, Delaware, 19804.

Ross House Books, P.O. Box 67, Vallecito, California, 95251.

Trinity Book Service, P.O. Box 131300, Tyler, Texas, 75713.

Tape Services

Chalcedon Audio-Visual Productions, P.O. Box 188, Vallecito, California, 95251.

Firestorm Chats, P.O. Box 8204, Fort Worth, Texas, 76124.

Geneva Ministries, P.O. Box 131300, Tyler, Texas, 75713.

L'Abri Cassettes, P.O. Box 2035, Michigan City, Indiana, 46360.

Mt. Olive Tape Library, P.O. Box 422, Mt. Olive, MS 39119.

Vorthos Tapes, P.O. Box 1141, Humble, Texas, 77347.

Newsletters

American Vision, P.O. Box 720515, Atlanta, Georgia, 30328.

Chalcedon Report, P.O. Box 158, Vallecito, California, 95251.

Christian Worldview, P.O. Box 1141, Humble, Texas, 77338.

ClipNotes, P.O. Box 8204, Fort Worth, Texas, 76124.

Coalition of Unregistered Churches, 2560 Sylvan Rd., East Point, Georgia, 30344.

Geneva Review, P.O. Box 131300, Tyler, Texas, 75713.

Forerunner, P.O. Box 1799, Gainesville, Florida, 31602.

Intercessors for America, P.O. Box 2639, Reston, Virginia, 22090.

Institute for Christian Economics, P.O. Box 8000, Tyler, Texas, 75701.

Plymouth Rock Foundation, P.O. Box 425, Marlborough, New Hampshire, 03455.

Remnant Review, P.O. Box 8204, Fort Worth, Texas, 76124.

Rescue, P.O. Box 1141, Humble, Texas, 77347.

Rutherford Institute Report, P.O. Box 5101, Manassas, Virginia, 22110.

Texas Christian Heritage Foundation. P.O. Box 162726, Austin, Texas, 78716.

Texas Grassroots Coalition, 95001 Capitol of Texas North, #304, Austin, Texas, 78759.

Washington Report, P.O. Box 8204, Fort Worth, Texas, 76124.

Magazines and Journals

Christianity and Civilization, P.O. Box 131300, Tyler, Texas, 75713.

Chronicles of Culture, 934 Main St., Rockford, Illinois, 61103.

Communication Institute, P.O. Box 612, Champaign, Illinois, 61820.

Counsel of Chalcedon, P.O. Box 888022, Atlanta, Georgia 30338.

Conservative Digest, P.O. Box 2246, Fort Collins, Colorado, 80522.

Human Life Review, 150 E. 35th St.#840, New York, New York, 10016.

Insight, 3600 New York Avenue N.E., Washington, D.C., 20002.

New American, 395 Concord Avenue, Belmont, Massachussetts, 02178.

Candidates Biblical Scoreboard, P.O. Box 10428, Costa Mesa, California, 92627.

How to Become an Effective Grassroot Lobbyist, Free Congress Research and Education Foundation, 721 Second St. N.E., Washington, D.C., 20002.

Congressional Quarterly Weekly Report, NAE Office of Public Affairs, 1430 K Street N.W., Washington, D.C., 20005.

National Prayer Committee, P.O. Box 6826, San Bernadino, California, 92412.

Correspondence

A *Congressional Staff Directory* may be purchased at a cost of $25 prepaid from Congressional Staff Directory, P.O. Box 62, Mount Vernon, Virginia, 22121.

One of the many groups publishing voting records of Congressmen is the Committee for the Survival of a Free Congress, 721 2nd St. N.E., Washington, D.C., 20002.

A *Letterwriter's Guide to Congress*, Chamber of Commerce of the United States, 1615 H St. N.W., Washington, D.C., 20062.

White House Comment Line: 202-456-7639, Justice Department Busing Complaint Line: 202-633-3847, General Litigation Complaint Line: 202-633-4713.

Congressional Record, Superintendent of Documents, U.S. Government Printing Office, Washington, D.C., 20402; 202-783-3238.

U.S. Capitol Switchboard, 202-225-1771 from 7 A.M. to 11 P.M., seven days a week.

Legislative Information Office, 202-225-1772 from 7 A.M. to 11 P.M., seven days a week.

To listen to recorded messages on the latest legislative activity, call 202-224-8541 (for Senate Democrats); 202-244-8601 (for Senate Republicans); 202-225-7400 (for House Democrats); and 202-225-7430 (for House Republicans).

For $2 you can send a 15-word message (a personal opinion wire) to any legislator. The bill will be sent to you or put on your phone bill. Call your Western Union office.

SCRIPTURE INDEX

OLD TESTAMENT

Genesis		*Genesis*	
1:26	45	10:8-10	38
1:26-28	xii, 19, 135	10:22	104
1:26-31	109	11:1-4	38
1:28	22, 45, 61, 105	11:4	38
2:8	44, 45	12:1	44
2:9	45	12:1-3	103, 110
2:10	45	12:1-4	37, 103
2:10-14	45	12:2	43, 44
2:11	45	12:3	44
2:13	45	12:4-9	48, 49
2:14	45	12:7	44
2:15	37	12:8	49
2:16-25	109	13:2	48
3:1-20	37	13:9	57
3:7	45	13:10	38
3:17-19	45, 46	13:15	44
3:18	75	13:17	44
3:23	46	14:1	104
3:24	46	14:1-20	48
3:24-4:12	46	14:1-24	48
4:3-8	19	14:5-7	104
4:8	46	14:13-17	104
4:12	37, 46	14:14-17	71
4:14	46	14:22	8
4:16	37	15:1	43
4:17	38	15:1-21	95, 110
4:23-24	46	15:6	26
6:2-4	46	15:18-21	43, 104
6:5	46	17:4	43
7:17-24	46	17:7	43
9:1-17	110	17:8	44
9:25	104	18:11-14	103
9:25-27	104	18:16-22	35

169

NEW TESTAMENT

WHAT ARE BIBLICAL BLUEPRINTS?

by Gary North

How many times have you heard this one?

"The Bible isn't a textbook of . . ."

You've heard it about as many times as you've heard this one:

"The Bible doesn't provide blueprints for . . ."

The odd fact is that some of the people who assure you of this are Christians. Nevertheless, if you ask them, "Does the Bible have answers for the problems of life?" you'll get an unqualified "yes" for an answer.

Question: If the Bible isn't a textbook, and if it doesn't provide blueprints, then just how, specifically and concretely, does it provide answers for life's problems? Either it answers real-life problems, or it doesn't.

In short: *Does the Bible make a difference?*

Let's put it another way. If a mass revival at last hits this nation, and if millions of people are regenerated by God's grace through faith in the saving work of Jesus Christ at Calvary, will this change be visible in the way the new converts run their lives? Will their politics change, their business dealings change, their families change, their family budgets change, and their church membership change?

In short: Will conversion make a visible difference in our personal lives? If not, why not?

Second, two or three years later, will Congress be voting for a different kind of defense policy, foreign relations policy, environmental policy, immigration policy, monetary policy, and so forth?

Will the Federal budget change? If not, why not?

In short: Will conversion to Christ make a visible difference in our civilization? If not, why not?

The Great Commission

What the Biblical Blueprints Series is attempting to do is to outline what some of that visible difference in our culture ought to be. The authors are attempting to set forth, in clear language, *fundamental Biblical principles* in numerous specific areas of life. The authors are not content to speak in vague generalities. These books not only set forth explicit principles that are found in the Bible and derived from the Bible, they also offer specific practical suggestions about what things need to be changed, and how Christians can begin programs that will produce these many changes.

The authors see the task of American Christians just as the Puritans who came to North America in the 1630's saw their task: *to establish a city on a hill* (Matthew 5:14). The authors want to see a Biblical reconstruction of the United States, so that it can serve as an example to be followed all over the world. They believe that God's principles are tools of evangelism, to bring the nations to Christ. The Bible promises us that these principles will produce such good fruit that the whole world will marvel (Deuteronomy 4:5-8). When nations begin to marvel, they will begin to soften to the message of the gospel. What the authors are calling for is *comprehensive revival* — a revival that will transform everything on earth.

In other words, the authors are calling Christians to obey God and take up the Great Commission: to *disciple* (discipline) all the nations of the earth (Matthew 28:19).

What each author argues is that there are God-required principles of thought and practice in areas that some people today believe to be outside the area of "religion." What Christians should know by now is that *nothing* lies outside religion. God is judging all of our thoughts and acts, judging our institutions, and working through human history to bring this world to a final judgment.

We present the case that God offers *comprehensive salvation* — regeneration, healing, restoration, and the obligation of total social reconstruction — because the world is in *comprehensive sin*.

To judge the world it is obvious that God has to have standards. If there were no absolute standards, there could be no earthly judgment and no final judgment because men could not be held accountable.

(Warning: these next few paragraphs are very important. They are the base of the entire Blueprints series. It is important that you understand my reasoning. I really believe that if you understand it, you will agree with it.)

To argue that God's standards don't apply to everything is to argue that sin hasn't affected and infected everything. To argue that God's Word doesn't give us a revelation of God's requirements for us is to argue that we are flying blind as Christians. It is to argue that there are *zones of moral neutrality* that God will not judge, either today or at the day of judgment, because these zones somehow are *outside His jurisdiction*. In short, "no law-no jurisdiction."

But if God *does* have jurisdiction over the whole universe, which is what every Christian believes, then there must be universal standards by which God executes judgment. The authors of this series argue for God's *comprehensive judgment*, and we declare His *comprehensive salvation*. We therefore are presenting a few of His *comprehensive blueprints*.

The Concept of Blueprints

An architectural blueprint gives us the structural requirements of a building. A blueprint isn't intended to tell the owner where to put the furniture or what color to paint the rooms. A blueprint does place limits on where the furniture and appliances should be put — laundry here, kitchen there, etc. — but it doesn't take away our personal options based on personal taste. A blueprint just specifies what must be done during construction for the building to do its job and to survive the test of time. It gives direction to the contractor. Nobody wants to be on the twelfth floor of a building that collapses.

Today, we are unquestionably on the twelfth floor, and maybe even the fiftieth. Most of today's "buildings" (institutions) were designed by humanists, for use by humanists, but paid for mostly by Christians (investments, donations, and taxes). These "buildings" aren't safe. Christians (and a lot of non-Christians) now are hearing the creaking and groaning of these tottering buildings. Millions of people have now concluded that it's time to: (1) call in a totally new team of foundation and structural specialists to begin a complete renovation, or (2) hire the original contractors to make at least temporary structural modifications until we can all move to safer quarters, or (3) call for an emergency helicopter team because time has just about run out, and the elevators aren't safe either.

The writers of this series believe that the first option is the wise one: Christians need to rebuild the foundations, using the Bible as their guide. This view is ignored by those who still hope and pray for the third approach: God's helicopter escape. Finally, those who have faith in minor structural repairs don't tell us what or where these hoped-for safe quarters are, or how humanist contractors are going to build them any safer next time.

Why is it that some Christians say that God hasn't drawn up any blueprints? If God doesn't give us blueprints, then who does? If God doesn't set the permanent standards, then who does? If God hasn't any standards to judge men by, then who judges man?

The humanists' answer is inescapable: *man* does—autonomous, design-it-yourself, do-it-yourself man. Christians call this man-glorifying religion the religion of humanism. It is amazing how many Christians until quite recently have believed humanism's first doctrinal point, namely, that God has not established permanent blueprints for man and man's institutions. Christians who hold such a view of God's law serve as *humanism's chaplains*.

Men are God's appointed "contractors." We were never supposed to draw up the blueprints, but we *are* supposed to execute them, in history and then after the resurrection. Men have been given dominion on the earth to subdue it for God's glory. "So God created man in His own image; in the image of God He created him; male and female He created them. Then God blessed them, and God said to them, 'Be fruitful and multiply; fill the earth and subdue it; have dominion over the fish of the sea, over the birds of the air, and over every living thing that moves on the earth'" (Genesis 1:27-28).

Christians about a century ago decided that God never gave them the responsibility to do any building (except for churches). That was just what the humanists had been waiting for. They immediately stepped in, took over the job of contractor ("Someone has to do it!") and then announced that they would also be in charge of drawing up the blueprints. We can see the results of a similar assertion in Genesis, chapter 11: the tower of Babel. Do you remember God's response to that particular humanistic public works project?

Never Be Embarrassed By the Bible

This sounds simple enough. Why should Christians be embarrassed by the Bible? But they *are* embarrassed . . . millions of them. The humanists have probably done more to slow down the spread of the gospel by convincing Christians to be embarrassed by the Bible than by any other strategy they have adopted.

Test your own thinking. Answer this question: "Is God mostly a God of love or mostly a God of wrath?" Think about it before you answer.

It's a trick question. The Biblical answer is: "God is equally a God of love and a God of wrath." But Christians these days will generally answer almost automatically, "God is mostly a God of love, not wrath."

Now in their hearts, they know this answer can't be true. God sent His Son to the cross to die. His own Son! That's how much God hates sin. That's wrath with a capital "W."

But why did He do it? Because He loves His Son, and those who follow His Son. So, you just can't talk about the wrath of God without talking about the love of God, and vice versa. The cross is the best proof we have: God is both wrathful and loving. Without the fires of hell as the reason for the cross, the agony of Jesus Christ on the cross was a mistake, a case of drastic overkill.

What about heaven and hell? We know from John's vision of the day of judgment, "Death and Hades [hell] were cast into the lake of fire. This is the second death. And anyone not found written in the Book of Life was cast into the lake of fire" (Revelation 20:14-15).

Those whose names are in the Book of Life spend eternity with God in their perfect, sin-free, resurrected bodies. The Bible calls this the New Heaven and the New Earth.

Now, which is more eternal, the lake of fire, or the New Heaven and the New Earth? Obviously, they are both eternal. So, God's wrath is equally ultimate with His love throughout eternity. *Christians all admit this*, but sometimes only under extreme pressure. And that is precisely the problem.

For over a hundred years, theological liberals have blathered on and on about the love of God. But when you ask them, "What about hell?" they start dancing verbally. If you press them, they eventually deny the existence of eternal judgment. We *must* understand: they have no doctrine of the total love of God because they have no doctrine of the total wrath of God. They can't really understand what it is that God in His grace offers us in Christ because they refuse to admit what eternal judgment tells us about the character of God.

The doctrine of eternal fiery judgment is by far the most unacceptable doctrine in the Bible, as far as hell-bound humanists are concerned. They can't believe that Christians can believe in such a horror. But we do. We must. This belief is the foundation of Christian evangelism. It is the motivation for Christian foreign missions. We shouldn't be surprised that the God-haters would like us to drop this doctrine. When Christians believe it, they make too much trouble for God's enemies.

So if we believe in this doctrine, the doctrine above all others that ought to embarrass us before humanists, then why do we start to squirm when God-hating people ask us: "Well, what kind of God would require the death penalty? What kind of God would send a plague (or other physical judgment) on people, the way He sent one on the Israelites, killing 70,000 of them, even though they had done nothing wrong, just because David had conducted a military census in peacetime (2 Samuel 24:10-16)? What kind of God sends AIDS?" The proper answer: "The God of the Bible, *my* God."

Compared to the doctrine of eternal punishment, what is some two-bit judgment like a plague? Compared to eternal screaming agony in the lake of fire, without hope of escape, what is the death penalty? The liberals try to embarrass us about these earthly "down payments" on God's final judgment because they want to rid the world of the idea of final judgment. So they insult the character of God, and also the character of Christians, by sneering at the Bible's account of who God is, what He has done in history, and what He requires from men.

Are you tired of their sneering? I know I am.

Nothing in the Bible should be an embarrassment to any Christian. We may not know for certain precisely how some Biblical truth or historic event should be properly applied in our day, but every historic record, law, announcement, prophecy, judgment, and warning in the Bible is the very Word of God, and is not to be flinched at by anyone who calls himself by Christ's name.

We must never doubt that whatever God did in the Old Testament era, the Second Person of the Trinity also did. God's counsel and judgments are not divided. We must be careful not to regard Jesus Christ as a sort of "unindicted co-conspirator" when we read the Old Testament. "For whoever is ashamed of Me and My words in this adulterous and sinful generation, of him the Son of Man also will be ashamed when He comes in the glory of His Father with the holy angels" (Mark 8:38).

My point here is simple. If we as Christians can accept what is a very hard principle of the Bible, that Christ was a blood sacrifice for our individual sins, then we shouldn't flinch at accepting any of the rest of God's principles. As we joyfully accepted His salvation, so we must joyfully embrace all of His principles that affect any and every area of our lives.

The Whole Bible

When, in a court of law, the witness puts his hand on the Bible and swears to tell the truth, the whole truth, and nothing but the truth, so help him God, he thereby swears on the Word of God — the *whole* Word of God, and *nothing but* the Word of God. The Bible is a unit. It's a "package deal." The New Testament doesn't overturn the Old Testament; it's a *commentary* on the Old Testament. It tells us how to use the Old Testament properly in the period after the death and resurrection of Israel's messiah, God's Son.

Jesus said: "Do not think that I came to destroy the Law or the Prophets. I did not come to destroy but to fulfill. For assuredly, I say to you, till heaven and earth pass away, one jot or one tittle will by no means pass from the law till all is fulfilled. Whoever therefore breaks one of the least of these commandments, and teaches men to do so, shall be called least in the kingdom of heaven; but whoever does and teaches them, he shall be called great in the kingdom of heaven" (Matthew 5:17-19). The Old Testament isn't a discarded first draft of God's Word. It isn't "God's Word emeritus."

Dominion Christianity teaches that there are four covenants under God, meaning four kinds of *vows* under God: personal (individual), and the three institutional covenants: ecclesiastical (the church), civil (governments), and family. All other human institutions (business, educational, charitable, etc.) are to one degree or other under the jurisdiction of these four covenants. No single covenant is absolute; therefore, no single institution is all-powerful. Thus, Christian liberty is *liberty under God and God's law.*

Christianity therefore teaches pluralism, but a very special kind of pluralism: plural institutions under God's comprehensive law. It does not teach a pluralism of law structures, or a pluralism of moralities, for as we will see shortly, this sort of ultimate pluralism (as distinguished from *institutional* pluralism) is always either polytheistic or humanistic. Christian people are required to take dominion over the earth by means of all these God-ordained institutions, not just the church, or just the state, or just the family.

The kingdom of God includes every human institution, and every aspect of life, for all of life is under God and is governed by His unchanging principles. All of life is under God and God's principles because God intends to *judge* all of life *in terms of* His principles.

In this structure of *plural governments*, the institutional churches serve as *advisors* to the other institutions (the Levitical function), but the churches can only pressure individual leaders through the threat of excommunication. As a restraining factor on unwarranted church authority, an unlawful excommunication by one local church or denomination is always subject to review by the others if and when the excommunicated person seeks membership elsewhere. Thus, each of the three covenantal institutions is to be run under God, as interpreted by its lawfully elected or ordained leaders, with the advice of the churches, not the compulsion.

Majority Rule

Just for the record, the authors aren't in favor of imposing some sort of top-down bureaucratic tyranny in the name of Christ. The kingdom of God requires a bottom-up society. The bottom-up Christian society rests ultimately on the doctrine of *self*-government under God. It's the humanist view of society that promotes top-down bureaucratic power.

The authors are in favor of evangelism and missions leading to a widespread Christian revival, so that the great mass of earth's inhabitants will place themselves under Christ's protection, and voluntarily use His covenantal principles for self-government. Christian reconstruction begins with personal conversion to Christ and self-government under God's principles, then spreads to others through revival, and only later brings comprehensive changes in civil law, when the vast majority of voters voluntarily agree to live under Biblical blueprints.

Let's get this straight: Christian reconstruction depends on majority rule. Of course, the leaders of the Christian reconstructionist movement expect a majority eventually to accept Christ as savior. If this doesn't happen, then Christians must be content with only partial reconstruction, and only partial blessings from

God. It isn't possible to ramrod God's blessings from the top
down, unless you're God. Only humanists think that man is God.
All we're trying to do is get the ramrod away from them, and melt
it down. The melted ramrod could then be used to make a great
grave marker for humanism: "The God That Failed."

The Continuing Heresy of Dualism

Many (of course, not all!) of the objections to the material in
this book series will come from people who have a worldview that
is very close to an ancient church problem: dualism. A lot of well-
meaning Christian people are dualists, although they don't even
know what it is.

Dualism teaches that the world is inherently divided: spirit vs.
matter, or law vs. mercy, or mind vs. matter, or nature vs. grace.
What the Bible teaches is that this world is divided *ethically* and *personally*: Satan vs. God, right vs. wrong. The conflict between God
and Satan will end at the final judgment. Whenever Christians
substitute some other form of dualism for ethical dualism, they fall
into heresy and suffer the consequences. That's what has happened
today. We are suffering from revived versions of ancient heresies.

Marcion's Dualism

The Old Testament was written by the same God who wrote
the New Testament. There were not two Gods in history, meaning there was no dualism or radical split between the two testa-
mental periods. There is only one God, in time and eternity.

This idea has had opposition throughout church history. An
ancient two-Gods heresy was first promoted in the church about a
century after Christ's crucifixion, and the church has always re-
garded it as just that, a heresy. It was proposed by a man named
Marcion. Basically, this heresy teaches that there are two completely
different law systems in the Bible: Old Testament law and New
Testament law (or non-law). But Marcion took the logic of his
position all the way. He argued that two law systems means two
Gods. The God of wrath wrote the Old Testament, and the God of
mercy wrote the New Testament. In short: "two laws-two Gods."

Many Christians still believe something dangerously close to Marcionism: not a two-Gods view, exactly, but a God-who-changed-all-His-rules sort of view. They begin with the accurate teaching that the ceremonial laws of the Old Testament were fulfilled by Christ, and therefore that the *unchanging principles* of Biblical worship are *applied differently* in the New Testament. But then they erroneously conclude that the whole Old Testament system of civil law was dropped by God, and *nothing Biblical was put in its place*. In other words, God created a sort of vacuum for state law.

This idea turns civil law-making over to Satan. In our day, this means that civil law-making is turned over to humanists. *Christians have unwittingly become the philosophical allies of the humanists with respect to civil law.* With respect to their doctrine of the state, therefore, most Christians hold what is in effect a two-Gods view of the Bible.

Gnosticism's Dualism

Another ancient heresy that is still with us is gnosticism. It became a major threat to the early church almost from the beginning. It was also a form of dualism, a theory of a radical split. The gnostics taught that the split is between evil matter and good spirit. Thus, their goal was to escape this material world through other-worldly exercises that punish the body. They believed in *retreat from the world of human conflicts and responsibility.* Some of these ideas got into the church, and people started doing ridiculous things. One "saint" sat on a platform on top of a pole for several decades. This was considered very spiritual. (Who fed him? Who cleaned up after him?)

Thus, many Christians came to view "the world" as something permanently outside the kingdom of God. They believed that this hostile, forever-evil world cannot be redeemed, reformed, and reconstructed. Jesus didn't really die for it, and it can't be healed. At best, it can be subdued by power (maybe). This dualistic view of the world vs. God's kingdom narrowly restricted any earthly manifestation of God's kingdom. Christians who were influenced by gnosticism concluded that God's kingdom refers only to the institutional church. They argued that the institutional church is the *only* manifestation of God's kingdom.

This led to two opposite and equally evil conclusions. *First,* power religionists ("salvation through political power") who accepted this definition of God's kingdom tried to put the institutional church in charge of everything, since it is supposedly "the only manifestation of God's kingdom on earth." To subdue the supposedly unredeemable world, which is forever outside the kingdom, the institutional church has to rule with the sword. A single, monolithic institutional church then gives orders to the state, and the state must without question enforce these orders with the sword. The hierarchy of the institutional church concentrates political and economic power. *What then becomes of liberty?*

Second, escape religionists ("salvation is exclusively internal") who also accepted this narrow definition of the kingdom sought refuge from the evil world of matter and politics by fleeing to hide inside the institutional church, an exclusively "spiritual kingdom," now narrowly defined. They abandoned the world to evil tyrants. *What then becomes of liberty?* What becomes of the idea of God's progressive restoration of all things under Jesus Christ? What, finally, becomes of the idea of Biblical dominion?

When Christians improperly narrow their definition of the kingdom of God, the visible influence of this comprehensive kingdom (both spiritual and institutional at the same time) begins to shrivel up. The first heresy leads to tyranny *by* the church, and the second heresy leads to tyranny *over* the church. Both of these narrow definitions of God's kingdom destroy the liberty of the responsible Christian man, self-governed under God and God's law.

Zoroaster's Dualism

The last ancient pagan idea that still lives on is also a variant of dualism: matter vs. spirit. It teaches that God and Satan, good and evil, are forever locked in combat, and that good never triumphs over evil. The Persian religion of Zoroastrianism has held such a view for over 2,500 years. The incredibly popular "Star Wars" movies were based on this view of the world: the "dark" side of "the force" against its "light" side. In modern versions of this ancient dualism, the "force" is usually seen as itself impersonal: individuals personalize either the dark side or the light side by "plugging into" its power.

There are millions of Christians who have adopted a very pessimistic version of this dualism, though not in an impersonal form. God's kingdom is battling Satan's, and God's is losing. History isn't going to get better. In fact, things are going to get a lot worse externally. Evil will visibly push good into the shadows. The church is like a band of soldiers who are surrounded by a huge army of Indians. "We can't win boys, so hold the fort until Jesus comes to rescue us!"

That doesn't sound like Abraham, Moses, Joshua, Gideon, and David, does it? Christians read to their children one of the children's favorite stories, David and Goliath, yet in their own lives, millions of Christian parents really think that the Goliaths of this world are the unbeatable earthly winners. Christians haven't even picked up a stone.

Until very recently.

An Agenda for Victory

The change has come since 1980. Many Christians' thinking has shifted. Dualism, gnosticism, and "God changed His program midstream" ideas have begun to be challenged. The politicians have already begun to reckon with the consequences. Politicians are the people we pay to raise their wet index fingers in the wind to sense a shift, and they have sensed it. It scares them, too. It should.

A new vision has captured the imaginations of a growing army of registered voters. This new vision is simple: it's the old vision of Genesis 1:27-28 and Matthew 28:19-20. It's called *dominion*.

Four distinct ideas must be present in any ideology that expects to overturn the existing view of the world and the existing social order:

A doctrine of ultimate truth (permanence)
A doctrine of providence (confidence)
Optimism toward the future (motivation)
Binding comprehensive law (reconstruction)

The Changing of the Guard

The Marxists have had such a vision, or at least those Marxists who don't live inside the bureaucratic giants called the Soviet Union and Red China. The radical (please, not "fundamentalist") Muslims of Iran also have such a view.

Now, for the first time in over 300 years, Bible-believing Christians have rediscovered these four points in the theology of Christianity. For the first time in over 300 years, a growing number of Christians are starting to view themselves as an army on the move. This army will grow. This series is designed to help it grow. And grow tougher.

The authors of this series are determined to set the agenda in world affairs for the next few centuries. We know where the permanent answers are found: in the Bible, and *only* in the Bible. We believe that we have begun to discover at least preliminary answers to the key questions. There may be better answers, clearer answers, and more orthodox answers, but they must be found in the Bible, not at Harvard University or on the CBS Evening News.

We are self-consciously firing the opening shot. We are calling the whole Christian community to join with us in a very serious debate, just as Luther called them to debate him when he nailed the 95 theses to the church door, over four and a half centuries ago.

It is through such an exchange of ideas by those who take the Bible seriously that a nation and a civilization can be saved. There are now 5 billion people in the world. If we are to win our world (and these billions of souls) for Christ we must lift up the message of Christ by becoming the city on the hill. When the world sees the blessings by God upon a nation run by His principles, the mass conversion of whole nations to the Kingdom of our Lord will be the most incredible in of all history.

If we're correct about the God-required nature of our agenda, it will attract a dedicated following. It will produce a social transformation that could dwarf the Reformation. This time, we're not limiting our call for reformation to the institutional church.

This time, we mean business.

Geneva Ministries
P.O. Box 131300
Tyler, TX 75713

Gentlemen:

   I just finished reading George Grant's *The Changing of the Guard*.
I understand that your organization makes available several
newsletters that include articles by Rev. Grant, as well as articles
by James B. Jordan, Ray Sutton, and Gary DeMar. Please send
me additional information and put me on your mailing list.

_____
name

_____
address

_____
city, state, zip

_____
area code and phone number

☐ Enclosed is a tax-deductible donation to help meet expenses.

HELP Services
P.O. Box 1141
Humble, TX 77347

Gentlemen:

   I read about your organization in George Grant's book, *The
Changing of the Guard*. I want to subscribe to your newsletter *Glean-
ings*. Enclosed is a gift to cover the cost of printing and postage.

_____
name

_____
address

_____
city, state, zip

_____
area code and phone number

☐ Also, please send me more information about your other publica-
tions, *The Texas Education Review* and *To the Work*.

☐ Please accept this enclosed gift of $_____ for your ongoing
work with the poor, needy, and unborn.

Dr. Gary North
Institute for Christian Economics
P.O. Box 8000
Tyler, TX 75711

Dear Dr. North:

I read about your organization in George Grant's book, *The Changing of the Guard.* I understand that you publish several newsletters that are sent out for six months free of charge. I would be interested in receiving them:

☐ *Biblical Economics Today*
    Christian Reconstruction
    and *Covenant Renewal*

Please send any other information you have concerning your program.

_____
name

_____
address

_____
city, state, zip

_____
area code and phone number

☐ Enclosed is a tax-deductible donation to help meet expenses.

Jesus said to "Occupy till I come." But if Christians don't control the territory, they can't occupy it. They get tossed out into cultural "outer darkness," which is just exactly what the secular humanists have done to Christians in the 20th century: in education, in the arts, in entertainment, in politics, and certainly in the mainline churches and seminaries. Today, the humanists are "occupying." But they won't be for long. *Backward, Christian Soldiers?* shows you why. This is must reading for all Christians as a supplement to the *Biblical Blueprints Series*. You can obtain a copy by sending $1.00 (a $5.95 value) to:

> Institute for Christian Economics
> P.O. Box 8000
> Tyler, TX 75711

_____
name

_____
address

_____
city, state, zip

_____
area code and phone number

The *Biblical Blueprints Series* is a multi-volume book series that gives Biblical solutions for the problems facing our culture today. Each book deals with a specific topic in a simple, easy to read style such as economics, government, law, crime and punishment, welfare and poverty, taxes, money and banking, politics, the environment, retirement, and much more.

Each book can be read in one evening and will give you the basic Biblical principles on each topic. Each book concludes with three chapters on how to apply the principles in your life, the church and the nation. Every chapter is summarized so that the entire book can be absorbed in just a few minutes.

As you read these books, you will discover hundreds of new ways to serve God. Each book will show you ways that you can start to implement God's plan in your own life. As hundreds of thousands join you, and millions more begin to follow the example set, a civilization can be changed.

Why will people change their lives? Because they will see God's blessings on those who live by His Word (Deuteronomy 4:6-8).

Each title in the *Biblical Blueprints Series* is available in a deluxe paperback edition for $7.95, or a classic leatherbound edition for $15.95.

The following titles are scheduled for publication:

- Liberating Planet Earth: An Introduction to Biblical Blueprints
- Ruler of the Nations: Biblical Blueprints for Governments
- Who Owns the Family?: Biblical Blueprints for Family/State Relations
- In the Shadow of Plenty: Biblical Blueprints for Welfare and Poverty
- Honest Money: Biblical Blueprints for Money and Banking
- The Children Trap: Biblical Blueprints for Education
- Inherit the Earth: Biblical Blueprints for Economics
- The Changing of the Guard: Biblical Blueprints for Political Action
- Healer of the Nations: Biblical Blueprints for International Relations
- Second Chance: Biblical Blueprints for Divorce and Remarriage

Please send more information concerning this program.

_____
name

_____
address

_____
city, state, zip

Dominion Press • P.O. Box 8204 • Ft. Worth, TX 76124